God of Surprises

God of Surprises

GERARD W. HUGHES

Paulist Press
New York/Mahwah

First published in Great Britain by Darton, Longman & Todd, Ltd.

ISBN: 0-8091-0379-6

Published by Paulist Press
997 Macarthur Boulevard
Mahwah, N.J. 07430

Printed and bound in the United States of America.

In gratitude to all with whom
I have walked the inner journey

Contents

Acknowledgement

The scriptural quotations are taken from *The Jerusalem Bible*, published and copyright 1966, 1967 and 1968 by Darton, Longman and Todd Ltd and Doubleday & Co. Inc., by permission of the publishers.

Preface

Nine years ago I wrote a book called *In Search of a Way* describing two journeys, the one an 1100-mile walk from London to Rome, the other the journey in which we are all engaged, which began at our conception and ends with our death.

This is a guidebook for the second journey which we are all making. It is written especially for bewildered, confused or disillusioned Christians, who have a love-hate relationship with the Church to which they belong, or once belonged.

I am a Catholic, a priest and a Jesuit. Many people still think that Catholic priests, perhaps Jesuits especially, never suffer confusion, bewilderment or disillusion. I do.

I used to think such negative feelings were a sign of failure which I must overcome, or at least ignore if I were to remain a Jesuit priest. Now I realize how wrong I was, for God is the God of surprises who, in the darkness and the tears of things, breaks down our false images and securities. This in-breaking can feel to us like disintegration, but it is the disintegration of the ear of wheat: if it does not die to bring new life, it shrivels away on its own.

Through this painful in-breaking of the God of surprises, truths of Christian faith with which I was familiarly bored, or doubted, began to take on new meaning. As God breaks down the cocoon of our closed minds, he enters it. He is no longer remote and out there, no longer dwells only in tabernacles and temples of stone, but we meet him smiling at us in our bewilderment, beckoning to us in our confusion and revealing himself in our failure and disillusion as our only rock, refuge and strength.

Our minds contain many layers of consciousness. Breaking into a new layer is always threatening at first because we naturally fear what we do not know. The God who calls us to meet him is 'the ground and granite of our being'. Our journey through these layers of consciousness will always be accompanied by some measure of uncertainty, pain and confusion. These negative feelings are the nudgings of God. The facts are kind, and God is in the facts.

Christ said, 'The kingdom of heaven is like treasure hidden in a field which someone has found; he hides it again, goes off happy, sells everything he has and buys the field' (Matt. 13:44).

This book has only one purpose – to suggest some ways of detecting the hidden treasure in what you may consider a most unlikely field, yourself.

Most guide books make heavy reading unless we see the objects or visit the places described, and they can only be read slowly. This guide book for the inner journey is no exception. At the end of each chapter there are exercises so that readers may make their own journey. What you discover for yourself is more important and valuable than anything I have written. That is why the book does not attempt detailed descriptions, but limits itself to providing signposts.

The inner journey is not linear; the route spirals through our layers of consciousness. At one level of consciousness I may have journeyed towards the God of surprises, yet at a deeper level I may realize that I have hardly begun and must consult the guidebook again.

Some readers familiar with the inner journey will be more interested in some stages than in others, so here is a summary of the contents based on the parable of the treasure in the field:

Chapter 1 gives examples illustrating the truth that the treasure is within each of us.

Chapter 2 describes stages of the journey before we reach the field where the treasure is hidden.

Chapter 3 describes the field which contains the treasure, but it turns out to be a jungle inhabited by wild animals and ogres disguised as God.

Chapter 4 suggests ways of discovering paths through the jungle to the treasure – some methods of prayer.

Chapter 5 shows how the journey is not only made with our minds and with the religious part of ourselves, but involves our whole being and affects every aspect of it, our relations to other people, our attitude to health, wealth, reputation, power, and our reactions to the economic, social and political structures in which we live. This chapter locates the treasure more precisely.

Chapter 6 is on beginning to dig for the treasure and breaking through the first layer. The chapter is a commentary on Christ's 'Repent and believe the good news'.

Chapter 7 suggests some practical methods of digging through this first layer.

Chapter 8. When people begin to dig, they often become disheartened, discovering the first layer is harder and deeper and that they are weaker and more helpless than they thought. This chapter considers these difficulties and offers suggestions for coping with them.

Chapter 9 is on recognizing the treasure when we find it. Christ is the treasure. The Jews did not recognize him; we still fail to recognize him. This truth is illustrated in a letter written by an imaginary parish priest complaining of the disruptive behaviour of one of his parishioners.

Chapter 10 is on opening up the treasure – coming to know Christ. It points to a basic pattern in Christ's life, and therefore in ours too, which is revealed in the Gospels.

Chapter 11 is on recognizing Christ's passion, death and resurrection in the sorrows and joys of our own lives.

Chapter 12. We move towards the field and dig towards the treasure through the decisions we make in everyday life. This chapter is not a treatise on decision-making, but it offers some basic guidelines for individual and group decisions.

Chapter 13. The themes of the book are applied to a fear which haunts all of us, the threat of nuclear war.

I dedicate this book in gratitude to all with whom I have walked the inner journey and who taught me by sharing their own inner experience. I am grateful to Darton, Longman and Todd, the publishers, and, in particular, to Teresa de Bertodano and Victoria Wethered for their encouragement and patience in reading the early drafts of the book. I also thank those who sent me comment and criticism of early drafts and encouraged me to continue: Kay Caldwell, Cathy Campbell, Graham Chadwick, Charles Elliott, Liz Emery, Mary Rose Fitzsimmons, Michael Ivens, Brian McClorry, Anne McDowell, Michael Taylor.

Finally, I thank the Society of Jesus which introduced and guided me through the Spiritual Exercises of St Ignatius, which permeate this book, and Fr Jock Earle, the Jesuit Provincial, who gave me the time to write it.

Gerard W. Hughes

Where Your Treasure Is

I greet him the days I meet him, and bless when I understand.*
(G. M. Hopkins, 'The Wreck of the Deutschland')

The treasure is within you. In this chapter I shall give an example of a man who did begin to discover the treasure within himself and also some examples of people who had the treasure, but did not recognize it. We shall then look more closely at this inner life, its chaotic complexity, which refuses to be ignored, and how it affects every aspect of our individual and corporate life.

The Jesuit Order was founded in the sixteenth century by a Basque nobleman called Inigo of Loyola, later known as St Ignatius Loyola. Inigo was brought up in the Spanish court and emerged in his late twenties wild, lively, vain, ambitious, lustful, daring and courageous. He was aggressively orthodox. Even after his conversion he was planning to kill a Moor who, in casual conversation, had questioned Our Lady's virginity. Fortunately for the Moor, Inigo left the decision to his mule which, with better discernment than its master, took another road and the Moor lived on. Inigo's moral and devotional life did not match his orthodoxy.

In 1521 he was defending the city of Pamplona against French troops, who were very superior in numbers. The city governor wanted to surrender; but Inigo insisted on fighting on, until a cannon ball struck him, badly damaging his legs. The victors did their crude best for the wounded prisoner and

* This and other quotations from Gerard Manley Hopkins are taken from *Poems and Prose of Gerard Manley Hopkins*, ed. W. H. Gardner and N. H. Mackenzie, Oxford University Press for the Society of Jesus, London 1967.

sent him home to Loyola to recover. For months he lay in great pain, whiling away his time in daydreams which lasted three to four hours. He imagined the great deeds he would perform when better and the great lady whose love he would win, but the days were long and he asked for novels to distract him. Loyola castle did not have any novels, so he had to content himself with a Life of Christ by a Carthusian, Ludolph of Saxony, and with a collection of saints' lives. While reading these he began on a second series of daydreams, and now he was imagining himself outdoing the saints in their austerities. One saint, Humphrey of the desert, who seemed able to live on herbs, fresh air and prayer, particularly fascinated him. Inigo was now saying to himself, 'If Humphrey can do it, so can I. If Dominic and Francis can do it, so can I.' For weeks he alternated between the two kinds of daydream, until suddenly he noticed something which was to change not only his own life, but millions of other peoples' lives as well.

While both kinds of daydream were enjoyable at the time, he discovered that after he had dreamed of his great deeds and of the lady whose love he would win, he felt bored, empty and sad, but after dreaming of outdoing the saints he felt happy, hopeful and encouraged. He reflected on this differ-ence and so learned his first lesson in what later he was to call 'Discernment of Spirits', which we might term 'Distinguishing between our creative and our destructive inner moods and feelings'. This story of Inigo gives the beginnings of an answer to the question 'Where is our treasure?' The treasure lies hidden in our inner moods and feelings.

Before reading any further you may like to try looking at your own daydreams and then ask yourself the question, 'How do I feel at the end of them? Bored and empty, or hopeful and encouraged?' At this stage, do not attempt any analysis of what you may discover, but be content to notice the after-effects of your daydreams.

The next examples are of people who have great inner wealth but do not recognize it when they see it.

The first I shall call 'Jock', because he was a Scot, tall, sandy-haired, freckled and taciturn. By trade he was an interior decorator, but unemployed. I was staying with friends who were having a room decorated and Jock was helping for the day. He worked like a monk with a vow of silence, his conversation limited to an occasional 'Aye' or 'Mmm'. Before joining us for a meal, he went off for a pint or two and then had wine at the meal, but he still remained locked in his inner cell, adding only an occasional 'Ta' to the 'Ayes' and 'Mmms'. Towards the end of the meal we began talking about North Wales, where I was then working. Jock looked up from his plate with obvious interest, then he began to speak.

'Aye,' he said, 'Ah wis in Wales in the summer, ma first holiday away frae home.' I cannot now remember the details, for it was a long story. Either he had just been jilted by his girl friend and was trying to find her in North Wales, or he was trying to get away to forget her, but he continued, 'D'ye know whit ah found masel' doin'? Walkin' the bloody moors wi' a wee dug. Ma mates wid've thought ah wis crazy, but ah felt happy. Ah came tae cliffs by the sea and jist sat there. The sea looked affie big and ah felt very wee, but ah wis happy. Daft, isn't it? Ah cannie tell ma mates, 'cos they'd think ah wis kinky.'

Jock had a natural sense of wonder. He had a felt knowledge of his own tininess in face of creation, but experienced happiness, not terror. Wonder is the beginning of wisdom, and the happiness he felt was a taste of the joy of humility, which is a glad acceptance of our tininess and dependence. He could be absorbed by the scene from the cliff top and showed no desire to manipulate it or control it, so he has the beginnings of the gift of contemplation, but an undue regard for the opinion of his mates was likely to stifle any growth in him. Jock did not consider himself a religious or spiritual person. He was aware of the joy which his gift of wonder and ability to contemplate gave him, but he did not recognize it as a gift, was rather ashamed of it and so was unlikely to nurture it and let it lead him into a fuller life.

'Jane' was a university student about to go to Spain for a year as part of her degree course in modern languages. She came to see me, obviously upset. When I asked what was wrong, she said she was worried about feeling so happy at the prospect of Spain for a year. I was mystified, but having recently done a counselling course I echoed, as instructed, 'so you are worried at looking forward to the year in Spain?' 'Yes,' she replied, 'but it is the reason for my happiness which is worrying me. In Spain I won't have to pretend to be a Catholic any more and I can miss going to Mass without offending my parents and having rows at home.' 'So the reason you continue to go to Mass and pretend to be a Catholic is that you want to avoid trouble with your parents?' 'And relatives and some other Catholic friends,' she added. I asked her what she hoped to do after her degree course and she said she wanted to go and teach in Peru. She wanted Peru because she had read about the country, had seen some documentary films and knew that there was great poverty and poor educational facilities for peasant children there. 'I have received so much,' she said, 'that I want to share something of what I have received with those who have little or nothing.' 'Have you ever thought that you have a vocation from God?' I asked. 'Don't be daft,' was her reply. Jane was quite certain that there was nothing religious in what she was experiencing. Religion for her was going to Mass on Sundays and observing the other rituals laid down by the Church. To be religious or spiritual, in her understanding of those terms, meant understanding and appreciating the teachings of the Catholic Church. She found Mass a meaningless bore and the teachings of the Church, as she understood them, to be statements about a world which had no meaning for her. She wanted to drop the lot and live, but she was not yet strong enough inside to live out her convictions. She thought of herself as irreligious and unspiritual, yet her dominant emotion was compassion; she wanted to share what she had been given and, in gratitude for what she had received, she wanted to serve. Her desire to be compassionate, to share and to serve echoed St Paul's description of Christ, who 'did not cling to his equality with God, but emptied himself to assume the condition of a slave, and became as men are . . .' (Phil. 2:6–7). Jane had more to be grateful for than she realized, yet such was her notion of God, the Church and religion, that she considered herself irreligious and estranged from the Church.

Recently I have had weekend meetings with an organization called The Association of Divorced and Separated Catholics, encouraging them to talk together about their experience of being divorced or separated. On the first weekend I was nervous at the intensity of emotion in the group. Some

4

were still seething with rage against their former partners and against the Church which had now left them doomed to an unwanted celibacy for the rest of their lives or, if they did remarry, to exclusion from the sacraments of the Church. Others had gone a stage further and were too wounded with self-doubt to rage at anyone or anything. They had loved and trusted their partners. Their trust had been betrayed, their love turned sour, and they had entered the worst stage of all, the experience of their own emptiness and nothingness, the threshold of despair with its door to suicide. They felt themselves to be failures and considered it useless to try to pray, because they felt they had failed God as well as themselves and their partner. Religion had so been presented that far from enabling them to understand and grow through their agony, it intensified the pain, guilt and sense of rejection, assuring them that they had not only lost their partner and split their family, but that they were also living in a state of alienation from God.

I knew that I had no answers for this group, but they ministered to one another. The most battered were often the most helpful. There was no judging one another, no rejection or intolerance, no pretence at virtue, but simply an acknowledgement of pain and a staying with one another in it. Put into Christian language, they were being Christs to one another, allowing themselves to be channels of his peace, compassion and hope. Out of their experience of death, they began to experience something of his risen life strengthening them to face the future with hope. With many of them, however, God and Christ were distant and unreal figures who could not possibly enter their lives except to condemn them and add to their feelings of rejection.

A few years ago, I had to travel regularly from North Wales to London and I gave lifts to hitch-hikers when I could. I did not wear clerical dress, nor let them know that I was a priest unless they asked. I tried to get them talking about themselves, their hopes and ambitions. Apart from one Jehovah's Witness, who spent the journey trying to convert me, I can remember none who was practising any form of religion. Most were hard up, but none seemed preoccupied with money. They disliked the rat race and were looking for something worthwhile in their lives. 'I want to be of some use to people,' was a constant refrain. Many people tirade against the materialism and unspirituality of our age, but spirituality has been interpreted so narrowly that we do not recognize it when we meet it in ourselves and in others.

I have given these examples as illustrations of the value of our own inner experience, which can tell us the direction our lives should take and supply the inspiration and energy to take it. Inigo reflected on his own experience, slowly learned how to interpret it and so transformed his own life, and has affected the lives of millions of other people. In the other examples, all the people mentioned had great inner wealth, but they did not recognize its value. In some cases they misread it, and in no case did they consider what they were experiencing to have anything to do with God, or Christ; yet it is in that inner experience that they were meeting God.

Everyone has this rich, complex inner life of thoughts, memories, feelings and desires. Its composition is unique to each of us, the result of our heredity and of all that we have done and all that has been done to us. There is no experience of our lives which does not register somehow in our body and in our mind. Most of our past experience is buried so deep in our memory that it is no longer accessible to our conscious mind, but these hidden memories still affect our perception of the world around us and so influence the way in which we act and react.

It is astonishing that we pay so little attention to this inner life, the key to our behaviour. We are like riders on wild horses. They rear, plunge and swerve. We have no idea why they are behaving in this way ('I don't know what came over me. I don't know why I did it'), and spend all our energy and ingenuity on trying to keep in the saddle, bucking our painful way through life. The obvious answer is to understand and befriend the horse, but we belong to a race of riders who consider such an approach to be slightly morbid and unscientific. In our ethos the horse must be ignored and we must ride with a stiff upper lip. I am told that in the Royal Navy only ratings are allowed to have emotions: officers are above that kind of thing! But even in religious circles one can still hear the advice, 'Pay no attention to your feelings'.

The horse is our inner life, source of our direction and energy for the journey through life, but we tend to ignore it because the inner life cannot be measured quantitatively, assuming, as we do, that it is numbers, not love, which makes the world go round. We have divinized reason and quantity, brutalized emotion and quality; and emotion, like a neglected child, takes a hideous revenge. Unless acknowledged and befriended, the neglected emotions will destroy us.

A large number of hospital beds in Britain are occupied by psychiatric patients. Western medicine, which for so long treated the body as though it were a machine curable without reference to the inner life of the patient (just as a car can be repaired without having to repair the driver at the same time), is now becoming increasingly aware of the close and intricate connection between bodily illness and the inner disharmony of the mind and the emotions. While it is not true to say that every bodily illness can be cured if the inner harmony of mind and heart can be restored, it is true to say that many, perhaps the majority of bodily illnesses, are the expression of inner disharmony. Resentment and bitterness over past hurts, frustration at the thwarting of our desires, can express themselves in arthritic conditions, in cancer, coronaries and other fatal diseases.

In public life we are obsessed with questions of the economy, a quantitative science, and with national defence, which has also become a quantitative science. We must have more destructive weaponry than 'they' have, in order to preserve our freedom. But there can be no freedom as long as we ignore our inner life. Inner disharmony in the individual expresses itself in bodily illness; inner disharmony in a nation expresses itself in various forms of national sickness. The inner life refuses to be ignored. It will give us no peace and may even destroy us if it is not acknowledged and befriended.

I have not kept in touch with 'Jock', the decorator, and so I do not know how he reacted to his experience by the sea, but let us suppose he ignored it as something which his friends would consider 'kinky', and he decides to admit only those feelings which his friends would consider acceptable. He has decided to ignore a deep part of himself, renounced his own rich individuality, his own freedom to act and to be as he really wants to be, and has chosen instead to conform to that pattern of behaviour which will win the approval of his mates. He may try to forget his feelings of peace and contentment on the moors and by the sea, but the experience, and the desires within him which that experience answered, will live on, if not in his conscious, then in his subconscious mind, and will express themselves in feelings of frustration, discontent and restlessness. He may fall into a depression but will not know its cause. He will go to the doctor and receive tranquillizers, as thousands of other people do. The tranquillizers may lessen the intensity of his depression, but they also muffle the message his body is giving, and so he is less likely than ever to discover the true cause of his sadness. The facts are kind, for these feelings of frustration and depression are nudging him to change his way of life. Even in the blackest mood, when a person is tempted to suicide, the facts are kind, for the depression is not saying, 'take your own life', but 'your present style of life is intolerable'.

We are tempted to ignore our inner life because we do not like what we find there. Take, for example, a mother who experiences strong dislike for her child, but is so ashamed of having such feelings that she will not acknowledge them even to herself. She pretends she has no such feelings, protests her great affection too much, peppering her conversation with 'darling', and convinces herself that she is a model mother. But the dislike, unless acknowledged, will find an outlet and the child will pick it up. The mother may become over-protective, possessive and dominating, and may reproach the recalcitrant child with 'How can you be so ungrateful after all that I have done for you?' In fact, she is damaging her child. Had she been able to acknowledge her dislike, then she might have seen that dislike is a very natural reaction to the child at times, but that may be a very superficial feeling compared with her deeper levels of genuine affection.

When the inner life is ignored, violence erupts in some form or other, whether in physical or mental illness in the individual, or civil unrest within a nation, or war between nations.

To sum up this chapter so far:

Our treasure lies in our inner life. It is our inner life which affects our perception of the world and determines our actions and reactions to it. We tend to ignore this inner life, but it refuses to be ignored either in individual or in national life. If ignored, the inner life will erupt in some form of violence.

In religious language this inner life is called 'the soul', and the art of knowing it, healing it and harmonizing its forces is called spirituality. Religion should encourage us to become more aware of this inner life and should teach us how to befriend it, for it is the source of our strength and storehouse of our wisdom. Religion, as it is often presented and understood, not only fails to nurture this awareness, but sometimes even actively discourages it. This failure in teaching and understanding is the source of much of the confusion, bewilderment and disillusion which besets so many Christians today, leading one writer to declare: 'Nothing so masks the face of God as religion.' In the next chapter we shall look more closely at this failure and the reasons for it, and so attempt to clear the approaches to the field where our treasure lies hidden.

Exercises

1. Examine the after-effects of your own daydreams, as suggested on page 2.
2. Write your own obituary notice. This may seem an odd and morbid suggestion, but try it first before deciding it is a waste of time.

   Do not write the obituary which you are afraid you might have, but the kind of obituary which, in your wildest dreams, you would love to have. Do not analyse it, or try to think it out too clearly, but allow your fancy to run free. Having once done it, return to it now and again and see if you want to add to it or correct it.

   This can be a very useful exercise for getting more in touch with your inner life, above all with your desires which, as we shall see later, are at the core of our inner lives and determine their direction.

2

Clearing the Approaches

When I was a child, I used to talk like a child, and think like a child, and argue like a child, but now I am a man, all childish ways are put behind me. (1 Cor. 13:11)

The treasure lies in what you may consider a most unlikely field – yourself. It takes most of us a long time and we have many obstacles to overcome before we begin to recognize the field where our treasure is hidden, that is, before we learn to find and accept ourselves, where God is. Until we do find ourselves, God remains remote, a shadowy figure, to some unimportant, to others terrifying.

When I was a child, aged about three years, I was being put to bed one evening by one of my older sisters. I sat on the edge of the bed and uttered the word 'God'. I can still remember why I did it. I wanted to see what would happen.

Each evening at home all the family prayed the rosary before going to bed, kneeling on the floor of the sitting room facing the fireplace. Above the fireplace was a painting of Grandma in a heavy frame. She wore a hat which looked like a rock garden with a veil hanging from it making her face look very sad and mysterious. At prayer time I used to become afraid of this picture, fearing that Grandma might start moving in response to our prayers.

Judging from these early memories, I think God for me in childhood was a mysterious, remote, unpredictable but powerful figure, an impression confirmed later when, at the age of seven, I had to learn by heart the Catechism description of God as 'the Supreme Spirit who alone exists of Himself and is infinite in all perfections', a definition which set him well apart from anything in my experience. The danger is that he remains apart.

It is extraordinary that Christianity, which believes 'the Word became Flesh', should so emphasize the divinity of Christ that his humanity is so often neglected. We can only discover his divinity in and through his humanity, as his first disciples did. Unlike them, we cannot see and touch him in his humanity: we can only discover him in our own and other peoples'. Neglect of this truth and the attempt to bypass our humanity in our search for God is the root cause of much confusion, frustration and disillusion among Christians.

We find God in and through our human development. To illustrate this truth I shall draw on ideas contained in the first volume of a two-volume work by von Hügel, called *The Mystical Element in Religion*, which I have found very useful for understanding my own and other peoples' religious development.

Von Hügel takes the three main stages in human development – infancy, adolescence and adulthood – describing the predominant needs and activities which characterize each stage. He shows that religion must take account of and nurture the predominant needs and activities of each stage, and so concludes that religion must include three essential elements, an institutional element corresponding to the needs and activities of infancy, a critical element corresponding to adolescence, and a mystical element corresponding to adulthood. As he analyses each stage of growth, he is careful to show that the needs and activities of infancy do not disappear in adolescence, nor do the needs and activities of adolescence disappear in adulthood, but they should cease to be predominant if we are to grow into the following stage. He also shows the dangers inherent in each stage of growth. Religion must include all three elements, the institutional, the critical and the mystical. There is a constant danger that one element is over emphasized to the exclusion of the other two, or two elements are emphasized to the exclusion of the third, thus stifling the religious development of its members. Von Hügel applies this analysis to all world religions. In the summary, I shall restrict its reference to Christianity.

(When in this and the following chapters I write of 'the Church', unless specific mention is made of a particular Church, the word refers to all Churches, of whatever denomination, who believe 'Jesus is Lord'. In so using the word I am not making any assertion about those who are not explicitly Christian. As a Christian, I believe that God lives in and loves every single human being.)

In infancy our activities are predominantly concerned with physical movement and sense impressions and our needs are for food, warmth, protection and affection.

The medieval philosophers had a saying, 'Everything in the mind has its origin in the senses.' All human knowledge, including our knowledge of God, begins with sense impressions. If any of the child's senses are impaired, it is handicapped for life. Babies are laying solid foundations for their future education when they keep crawling along the floor touching and tasting everything they can lay their hands on, gurgling with delight as they shake their rattles, staring fixedly at bright colours, wanting to be held and to feel close to their mothers. Later, out of these sense impressions the child will make its most important educational leap when it begins to make signs and utter its first words. To deprive a child of sense impressions would be to cripple it for life. There is no stage of human development when we do not need sense impressions, but in adolescence and adulthood we should no longer need to spend hours crawling along the floor!

Once the child has begun to speak, it will repeat what it hears without, at first, understanding the meaning. Most children love the sound of rhyming words and their imagination is often so vivid that they have difficulty in distinguishing the imaginary from the real. I knew one child who would have a tantrum if a place were not laid at table for her non-existent friend, Frances. When a younger sister really did appear, she was also introduced to the non-existent Frances by her older sister, became equally attached and insisted on sitting on the other side of the invisible Frances at meal times, and this continued for about a year.

A child's memory must be stored with stories, with family and local history. Infants will normally accept as true whatever they are told by parents or anyone else. Without this initial credulity the learning process cannot begin. They must also be told what they may and what they may not do. To deprive a child of clear instruction and consistently to leave it to make up its own unformed and uninformed mind is cruelty. A very disturbed person, who had suffered a traumatic childhood, told me that one of her saddest memories was of playing with other children every evening and hearing them being called home one by one by their parents, but for her there was no call.

The greatest emotional needs in childhood are for protection and affection, for without these the child cannot learn to trust either itself or anyone else. The ability to grow humanly is proportionate to the ability to trust.

There are, of course, many other needs and activities in childhood. The child will begin to see patterns in sense perception and to interpret them, to ask questions and construct theories, but these activities are not dominant.

In the healthy adult the needs and activities of childhood continue to some extent. We always need sense perception, our memory has to be continually stored and restored, our imagination should be kept alive, we must be able to accept some authorities at least, and we need affection and attention no matter how adult we may be. However competent, we can never work out everything for ourselves and we must trust the competence of others. To have reached a stage of development when we no longer need affection and attention from anyone would be to have outgrown our humanity.

Christianity must minister to these human needs and encourage the activities of the child, emphasizing them particularly in childhood, but ensuring that they are also provided in adolescence and maturity. In leading us to God and presenting him to us in Word and Sacrament, the Church must speak not only to our minds, but also to our senses. We can only come to any knowledge, including our knowledge of God, through our sense impressions and then through signs and symbols. That is why the architecture, furnishings, the art in paintings and furnishings, the lighting, acoustics, the temperature of places of worship are so important and why the services need not only the beauty of words but also of music, gestures and movement. I know that this is anathema to some of the Reformed Churches with their horror of anything which smacks of idolatry, and I know, too, the danger that the externals of a Church and of its services, instead of helping to raise the mind and heart to the God we cannot see, may become an end in themselves, so that lighting a penny candle can become a substitute for having care of our neighbour, but that is a risk which must be taken. There is always the risk that a child will so enjoy the needs and activities of childhood that it becomes afraid to move to adolescence, but that is not a good reason for depriving it in childhood.

The Church, too, in childhood especially, but also later, must store our memories with the story of its history. As the family history is passed on to the child, the story of the Christian family must also be given, so that the child is introduced to the great stories of the Bible, the events of the Gospel and to the lives of the saints. There must be a teaching role in every religion. Children will normally accept whatever they are told as being true and are unlikely as infants to ask, 'On what do you base your assumptions that there is a God and why should I accept what you tell me as being true?' These problems begin later. Unless there is an acceptance stage, the child cannot learn to formulate questions because it will have nothing on which to base them.

The Church's teaching role is not limited to passing on factual information, but must also include moral teaching, for it would be cruel to leave a child to discover through trial and error what it may and may not do. The child has to be taught not to steal, not to lie, to keep the rice pudding on its plate and not stick it on the wall in a tantrum.

The Church must pass on to the child its history, its doctrinal and moral teaching in a way that the child can assimilate, but it must also continue this teaching role for the adolescent and adult, too. This statement is so obvious that it seems unnecessary to mention, yet this obvious truth has very often been ignored, children being instructed in a highly technical and abstract theological language on the one hand, and adults expected to accept this same mysterious language with the credulity of a child. Ministering to the predominant needs and activities of the child and continuing to minister to them in adolescents and adults constitutes the institutional element in the Church.

Although adolescence is normally characterized as the stage of growing sexual awareness, the awareness is more than sexual. Adolescence is the time when the mind begins to question. We are trying to discover some unity and meaning in the multiplicity of sense impressions, facts, teachings,

beliefs and experiences presented to us. The Greek philosophers were not the only ones to seek 'the One in the Many':
we all do it in our different ways.

At one time I had to teach religion to a bright class of 15-
year-olds, who had just finished their O-levels at Stonyhurst
College, a Jesuit boarding school. The school still insisted
that boys should attend Mass daily, so I prepared a course
on the history and development of the Mass, studied with
great care a heavy two-volume work by the German Jesuit
Jungmann, and tried to put it into digestible form for the
class. After five minutes of the opening class most of them
were wearing that glazed look reserved for chapel and
religious instruction. At the end, one of the class approached
me. 'Father,' he began, 'I suppose you realize you're wasting
your time.' I suspected he was right, but was not prepared
to admit it to him at that moment. 'Why do you say that?' I
asked. 'Because half of us are atheists,' was his reply. 'Which
half?' He paused, then said he would have to consult the
others before answering my question. 'By the way,' I said
'how long have you been atheist?' Solemnly he answered,
'About ten days'. Later in the day he came to me, having
consulted his atheist friends, and gave me a list of names.
'Would you call yourselves atheist', I asked, 'or agnostic?'
This distinction had not come into the O-level syllabus, so I
explained that the atheist rules out any possibility of God's
existence, while the agnostic does not assert either his existence, or non-existence. He decided that he and his friends,
being open-minded people, would be more correctly described
as agnostic.

We formed an Agnostics' Club and used to meet regularly
in their free time to discuss the question of God's existence.
One of the group had been reading Bertrand Russell and had
passed on the information to the others. They had decided
that all phenomena could be explained in terms of
bombarding particles of matter and that the key to all knowledge lay in discovering the mathematical formulae governing
the movement of these particles. In my room, where we used
to meet, there was a metal coal scuttle. At one meeting I
turned to one of them, a very serious youth, and asked, 'John,
do you really believe that the only real distinction between
your Mum and that coal scuttle lies in the different mathemat-

ical formulae governing the movement of their respective particles?' He sat, frowning with effort, then looked up, 'No, there's no difference,' he said. He was determined to stick by his theory and his friends.

This is a good example of the characteristic activity of adolescence, the search for meaning and unity in experience. We cannot live as human beings unless we can find some kind of unity and meaning in our lives. Even those who are labelled insane have some pattern of unity in their thinking and their acting, although the 'sane' may not be able to find it. The man who is paranoid may be totally mistaken in his basic assumption that the world is created to hunt him down but, given that assumption, his behaviour is logical and consistent. The most terrifying fear to which a human being can be subjected is the fear of annihilation and of meaninglessness, so we struggle with all our strength to find some kind of sense and meaning. The temptation is to settle for that theory of existence, or that pattern of meaning, which will ensure our material comfort and cause us the least inconvenience. If we are to develop as human beings we must find some unity in our experience, formulate some theory about our lives, however elementary and crude the theory may be; we must have some plans and dreams for the future and some idea of how to accomplish them, even if the plan is only to think as little as possible and ensure a minimum output of energy. To find meaning in our lives we have to question, criticize, systematize and theorize about our experience. This was the activity in which the Agnostics' Club were engaged and none of us can escape it, although we may try to do so.

The Church must answer this deep human need by evolving hypotheses and theories to show the coherence not only of its own teaching, but the coherence of its teaching with life as we experience it. A Church which concentrates simply on the coherence of its own teaching without relating it to everyday experience is behaving like the paranoid. There may be a coherence between the teaching and the practice of the Church, but if its basic assumptions are false, then there will be a disharmony between the teaching of the Church and our everyday life, and the teaching presented will split off and become a part of our consciousness which has nothing to do with the rest of our human experience. A Church

16

isolated from our human experience can only survive as long as it can succeed in forbidding its adherents to ask questions and think for themselves. It must lay heavy emphasis on the importance of obedience to religious authority, obedience being understood as unquestioning acceptance of whatever is presented by the teaching authority, and by making it sinful for its members to criticize, or to read or listen to anyone who may propose any contrary teaching.

A mark of true Christianity will be its intellectual vigour and its search for meaning in every aspect of life. True Christianity will always be critical, questioning and continually developing in its understanding of God and of human life. The subject matter for religion is every human experience. In Christian understanding, God is immanent, that is, he is present in all things, and creation itself is a sign, and an effective sign, of his presence – a sacrament. That is why there has been such an emphasis on scholarship and learning in the Christian tradition. Faith, as St Anselm wrote, 'seeks understanding', for it is the nature of true faith to trust that God is at work in everything and that there is no question which falls outside the scope of religious inquiry. When faith in God weakens, the critical element will also weaken, and there will be more warning against false doctrines than encouragement to develop our understanding. If the critical element is not fostered, Christians will remain infantile in their religious belief and practice, which will have little or no relation to everyday life and behaviour.

The characteristic of adulthood is a growing awareness of inner consciousness, of the complexity of feeling and emotion within us, revealed to us through our activity, our encounters and relationships with others, our work, what we read, hear and see, and of the internal activity which results from this, our hopes and despairs, sadness and joy, fears and expectations, certainties and doubts. As we become more conscious of this inner world, we are both attracted and frightened by it. We are coming closer to ourselves and, therefore, to God, experienced by the mystics as 'tremendum et fascinans', 'frightening, yet attractive'. This inner world is unique to each of us, mysterious and incommunicable even to ourselves in its complexity. Although we cannot understand this hidden world, we know that it holds the key to our happiness and to our personality, and that the way we perceive, think, and therefore act, has its explanation in this inner world, which exercises a much greater influence on us than any external circumstances. That is why different people faced with the same situation can act in such contrary ways. In adulthood, if we allow ourselves any time to think, we become increasingly conscious of the complexity of our inner life, of the mystery and incommunicability of it, and of the layers upon layers of consciousness within us.

Religion must answer this stage of our growth with encouragement and guidance, fostering our fascination and allaying our fears, explaining this phenomenon to us and showing us that this is a most important stage in our journey towards God, whom we are now invited to meet in these hidden, and often very frightening, recesses of our minds and memories – God, whose ways are not our ways and whose thoughts are not our thoughts, the God of surprises, who is now encountered rather than thought about, who communicates himself through these mysterious inner experiences rather than through the articulate phrases of set prayers, who is now being experienced from within rather than being presented from without, is loved and lived rather than theorized about, is action and power rather than any external constraint and discipline as in the institutional stage, or intellectual reasoning as in the critical. To help us in adulthood the Church must include a mystical element.

These three stages have been described successively, but each stage contains elements of the other two. In the child there is already the beginnings of the critical, and sometimes of the mystical stage. Similarly, in the critical stage there are still elements of the institutional and glimmerings of the mystical, but our attention has been on the needs and activities which predominate at each stage. In the adult, all three elements are present to some extent. When one or two elements are missing in the adult, there is imbalance in the personality. We shall now look again at these three stages, this time seeing more clearly the need and the inherent danger of each stage in life, and therefore also in religious development. We shall see, too, the effort which is required to move from one stage to the next and, in moving, the care that must be taken not to reject totally the stage we have just left. It is as though the journey through life was across a broad river and the bridge is built in three sections. We start along the institutional section, then move to the critical, but we shall be swept away by the river if we cut off all connection with the institutional section, even though it is not where we are standing at the moment. Similarly, on the mystical section of the bridge, we must keep our connection with the institutional and the critical.

The danger in the infancy stage of growth is inherent in its advantages. What is provided for us in infancy answers our most basic needs and allows us to be relatively passive while remaining protected and secure. The danger is that we find this stage so satisfactory that we are disinclined to move out of it, preferring to remain infantile. Even if we do move out, we may revert to infantilism if the following stages become too uncomfortable. We may even use our adult guile to get us back to being cared for like a child by feigning illness. If our deceit is successful enough, we may become seriously ill.

The danger in the institutional element in religion is that we never advance beyond a religious infantilism. We attend religious services, hear sermons and religious instructions, are told what is, and what is not, the Church's moral and doctrinal teaching, and the danger is that we may be content with this and desire to go no further, using, perhaps, our adult guile to justify us in our passivity. The way in which religion was often taught to Catholics, for example, since the Council of Trent in the sixteenth century, namely through a catechism of questions and answers, which were a summary of the very technical theological language contained in Trent's Council documents, encouraged Catholics to believe that religion is a subject which you are not expected to understand, but to which you must give your whole-hearted assent! This approach instilled a childish attitude with little or no encouragement to move beyond it. Much of the present tension within the Catholic Church is tension between those who assume that the institutional is the only essential element in the Church and others who are demanding more of the critical and mystical elements.

There is also a danger for those in authority in the Churches that they may encourage people to remain in the infantile stage, calling this retarded state 'being humble, loyal, faithful and observant', and threatening with the wrath of God anyone who dares to disagree. There is no more effective way of destroying true faith in God than by misusing words like loyalty, humility, obedience and faithfulness. These are important virtues which can help to keep us true and attentive to the promptings of God at work within us, but to use these virtues for the opposite purpose, namely to destroy any belief that God does work within our minds and hearts by assuring people that any disagreement with religious authorities must stem from their own sinfulness, so discouraging them from paying any attention to their own inner experience, the place of their encounter with God, is a sin and a scandal, and Christ has harsh words to say of those who scandalize children: 'It were better that a millstone were hung around their neck and they were thrown into the sea.'

The infantile attitude is not infrequently to be found in people who are not at all infantile in the ways of the world and who may be very prominent in public life. Their religion is sealed off so that it does not interfere with their career and the way they pursue it, and they are often the loudest in opposing any change in the Church. They want religion to be exactly as it was when they were children.

In adolescence, if we do not search for some kind of unity and meaning in our lives, we cannot begin to find any direction. We may be content to find enough unity to enable us to avoid immediate pain, and we may refuse to question any further through fear of what we may find. If we do continue to question and search for meaning, the danger is that this activity may threaten the security, protection and affection which we enjoyed in the infancy stage. Our searchings may lead us to reject the views of our parents and friends, which previously we accepted without question. The temptation to stop questioning is strong, because we need not only meaning in our lives, but also affection, support and protection from our family and friends. It is hard to keep on terms of close filial love when you believe, and let Mum and Dad know that you believe, that they are not essentially different from a coal scuttle!

In religion the same problem occurs. Criticizing and questioning can have most serious consequences, as the victims of the Inquisition knew with a felt knowledge. Questioning and criticism on religious matters can still break up marriage and family relations, can lead to exclusion from church member-ship and, in some countries, it can lead to long terms of imprisonment. I am not maintaining that everyone within a family, Church or nation should be allowed to believe and act out whatever they please while still being accepted as full members, but simply pointing out that questioning and criticism on religious matters can be very risky. It is good that it is so. If it did not matter what we believed, or how we acted out of those beliefs, then it would follow that religion is of no importance in everyday life. One of the signs that Christianity is vigorously alive in some parts of the world is the large number of Christians who are in prison for acting out their beliefs in their political options.

The Church must encourage the critical element in its members. If it fails to do so, then the individual will not be able to integrate religious belief with everyday experience or, put in other words, God will be excluded from most of the individual's life until religion comes to be considered a private but harmless eccentricity of a minority.

If the Church does encourage the critical element, then it must expect to be questioned and challenged by its members and it must be prepared to change its own ways of thinking and acting, submitting itself to the light of truth. Such an attitude is only possible in a Church which has a strong faith in God's presence in all things. Just as a child with strong trust in its parents is encouraged by that very trust to ask all kinds of questions, so a Church which really trusts God is not afraid, but encourages its members to search and ques-tion, guiding them in her wisdom and warning them of routes which she knows from long experience to be cul-de-sacs. Her teachings will never be delivered as the last word on any subject, but rather as signposts, encouraging her members to explore the route further for themselves.

If the critical element cuts loose from the institutional and the mystical, it will produce rationalists rather than religious people, whose devotion to a theological, moral, or philo-sophical system will take the place of their devotion to God. Such people will be suspicious of anything emotional and will advise others to ignore feelings. Those who cultivate the critical and neglect the other two elements will tend to be

21

rigid and dogmatic, with little to say to children and the uneducated, out of touch, too, with the child in themselves and with the mystery of their own inner thoughts and feelings, which are far too complex to be described adequately in abstract concepts. Such people are likely to be obsessed with the question of orthodoxy and the exposing of those whom they consider unorthodox.

The adult stage, with its increased inner awareness, is necessary because the source of all our thinking, desiring and willing, and therefore of our behaviour, is within us. If we are unwilling to come to know this inner world, we cannot come to know ourselves and therefore we cannot know the direction of our lives. If we neglect this inner world, or anaesthetize ourselves against it in some way, we shut ourselves off from God, from the source of our freedom, and so condemn ourselves to become non-persons.

The danger in this stage is that we become so absorbed in this inner world, its mystery and power, that we reject the institutional element in life, reject the traditions we have received, the authority we once accepted, and despise all abstract theologies and philosophies as being totally inadequate to express the richness of the reality we have discovered within.

Religion must encourage this inner awareness because it is in these inner experiences that we encounter the God of mystery, the God of surprises, whose Spirit is at work in our spirit in a manner unique to each individual. That is why instruction and guidance in prayer is even more essential for the adult Christian than doctrinal or moral instruction. Training in prayer should be the main preoccupation and service given by the bishops and clergy to the adult members of the Church.

The danger is that the mystical element may so be emphasized that the institutional and critical are neglected. This can lead to a rejection of formal prayer and worship, abandonment of moral and doctrinal teaching and the growth of an emotionalism which cannot be understood because it will not submit itself to the critical element. In the worst forms, the mystical element, unchecked and adrift from the institutional and critical, can produce wild extremism and dangerous fanaticism, and there is a long history of this religious madness in the life of the Church.

These then are the three essential elements in Christianity corresponding to the three stages of human growth. In each stage there is an innate tendency to reject the other two, or to form an alliance with one to the exclusion of the other. A common example is moving from the institutional to the mystical, bypassing the critical, a constant temptation in charismatic and pentecostal movements. All three elements are necessary, but an adult member or group within a Church may typify one element more than another, while not excluding the other two. Von Hügel mentions some of the great reforming popes as typifying the institutional element, St Thomas Aquinas as an example of the critical, and St John of the Cross as an example of the mystical. He also shows how some religious orders may emphasize one element more than another, describing Jesuits as examples of the institutional, Dominicans of the critical, and Benedictines of the mystical. He gives St Thomas More as an example of a man in whom all three elements were evenly blended.

The object of this analysis has been to clear the approaches to the field of our inner experience in which our treasure lies hidden. Many Christians, sometimes aided and abetted by their clergy, remain so firmly entrenched in the institutional element of the Church that they consider any venturing into the critical element to be disloyalty, a step towards unorthodoxy and loss of faith. Undue emphasis on the institutional element today is likely to produce a Church of dwindling numbers, loyal, obedient, docile, uninspired and passive members, God's frozen people.

A Church which encourages the critical as well as the institutional, but neglects the mystical element, will be intellectually alive but spiritually barren, its defenders as sharp as razors and about as broad. The spirit of prophecy will die in the Church and the deep symbolism of the institutional element's rites and rituals will lose their meaning, be questioned and rejected as irrelevant.

After reading this chapter, do not conclude that until you have completely overcome the infantilism of the institutional stage and the adolescence of the critical, that there is no hope of your entering the mystical. The object of this analysis is to help us spot the residual traces of infantilism and adolescence which are still preventing us from being adult in our faith. Recognizing these traces as they appear and resisting them is a movement towards inner freedom.

The remainder of this chapter consists of two exercises, the first to help assimilation of the von Hügel analysis, and the second is the writing of your own faith autobiography.

Exercises

1. On the Von Hügel analysis:

   (a) In your own experience of your Church, has any one element predominated to the exclusion of the other two, or have two elements been emphasized to the exclusion of a third?

   (b) Apply the same question to your own Christian life. Does the analysis help to clarify the reasons underlying your own feelings of confusion, bewilderment, disillusion? Are these feelings because you were satisfied with one element in the Church and you resent the introduction of the other two, or is it that you feel constricted in a Church which emphasizes one or other element to the exclusion of another?

   (c) In what ways, if any, does the analysis help you to understand some of the reasons which underlie current tensions and divisions within your Church and between the Churches.

2. Write your own faith autobiography.

   (The Old Testament may be described as a faith auto-biography of Israel. The Jews reflected on their history, a very messy and shameful history, with its brief moment of glory under King David, its long years of infidelity to God, of defeat, humiliation and captivity. They began to see their history in a new way, as a history of salvation in and through disaster and tribulation. Salvation history still continues in you and me. The Spirit who lived in Jesus and raised him from the dead, now lives in us and is at work in the events of our lives. To find God and to recognize our own history as a salvation history, we need to be in touch with our own history. This exercise is to help you get in touch with it.)

Ask yourself the question, 'What has God meant to me in my life?' As memories occur to you, scribble them down briefly, memories from childhood, from recent years, in any order.

If the question 'What has God meant to me?' does not elicit, but rather blocks memories, then change the question to 'What have been the important events, and who have been the important people in my life?'

Avoid, like the plague, any kind of self-judgement, whether approval or disapproval, or any attempt at analysis.

Once you begin this process, you will probably find that one memory evokes others. Jot them down as they occur to you in any order.

3

Inner Chaos and False Images of God

Every single time I want to do good, it is something evil that comes to hand. (Rom. 7:21)

The treasure is hidden within the field of our inner experience. As we reach adulthood, we become more aware not only of the field's mystery and complexity, but also of its dangers, and so the temptation is to ignore it. We may succeed, but our inner life will remain alive, influencing our behaviour, and often kicking vigorously.

In this chapter we shall look at the complexity and danger of our inner life, at the power and confusion of the drives and desires which are in us. Religious teachers tell us to turn to God in prayer if we are to find peace and harmony within. We shall apply the critical element to this advice and ask, 'Which God am I to turn to?'

Once we begin to look at our inner feelings we may begin to panic, for we may not like what we see and fear that some feelings may overwhelm and destroy us. Is it healthy to look at inner feelings? What if I find feelings of hate, resentment, bitterness, cruelty, destructiveness? If I advert to them and allow them entry into my consciousness, they may take over and lead me to do what I would rather not do. Am I not wiser to ignore them? If a priest, for example, vowed to celibacy, looks at his own desires and wants to marry, could this not wreck his life as a priest? If married people look at their desires and discover they do not want to be married, or not to this partner, is this not destructive of married life? Certainly, if whenever we looked at our desires we then followed the desire which first presented itself, our lives would be chaotic. We are a jumble of conflicting desires, and of

most of them we are not fully conscious, yet they are deter-
mining every decision of our lives. There is a very vivid
illustration of this conflict of desires in the Gospel, and the
story is so important that it is included in three of them – the
healing of the Gerasene demoniac.

Jesus has crossed the lake and no sooner has he got out of
the boat than a raving lunatic approaches. Mark (in chapter
5) describes the man in some detail. He lived among the
tombs and 'no one could secure him any more, even with a
chain'. There is a wild fury within the man which no fetters
can constrain. 'He had often been secured with fetters and
chains but had snapped the chains and broken the fetters,
and no one had the strength to control him.' The fury is
turned in on the man himself: 'All night and all day, among
the tombs and in the mountains, he would howl and gash
himself with stones.' The conflict within is destroying him.
When he sees Jesus, he runs up to him and shouts: 'What do
you want with me, Jesus, Son of the Most High God? Swear
by God that you will not torture me!' There are two movements within the man, one of attraction for Jesus, the other
of repulsion, and in the presence of Jesus both movements
are evoked. 'What is your name?' Jesus asks. With great
insight the man answers, 'My name is legion, for there are
many of us.'

The man is possessed by evil spirits which Jesus drives out
of him, and the scene ends with the man back in his senses,
fully clothed, sitting with Jesus and begging to be allowed to
stay with him. We may or may not believe in demonic
possession, but whatever our views may be, it is worth
pondering this passage and, while withholding any judgement
about the likelihood or unlikelihood of demonic possession,
trying to see our own inner lives in the light of this story.

Do we know what it is 'to live among the tombs', when life
seems to go dead and what once caused us pleasure and
delight now leaves us unmoved, so that we live in a state of
listlessness and apathy? Do we understand what it means 'to
howl and gash ourselves', for example with bitterness and
resentment at what others have done to us, or what we have
done to ourselves, the agony of feeling unforgiven, or of
refusing to forgive? Have we ever felt like legion, because we
can be so different from day to day and even within the same

day, now full of sweetness and light and goodwill to all, very reasonable and jovial; and a few minutes later something happens which leaves us glowering, unreasonable, a pain to ourselves and to anyone else who has the misfortune to come near? Do we recognize in ourselves the double movement in the demoniac who rushes up to Jesus on the one hand, and begs him depart on the other?

If we really could see into the depths of ourselves and into our subconscious and unconscious minds, we would recognize in ourselves all the characteristics of the demoniac and this would terrify us, but we would see also other qualities which would delight us. There is no crime, no perversion, no cruelty ever practised of which we are not capable, but there is also no heroism, selflessness or love which is beyond our potential. Because we are afraid of looking at the evil possibilities in us, we fail also to see our true greatness. Refusing to look at our inner lives, we ignore our true selves, renounce our individuality, our freedom, our personality, or, as the Jerusalem Bible puts it, 'we lose our very selves'.

One way in which we avoid looking at our own inner chaos and destructiveness is by projecting it on to other people. This habit of projecting blame on to others is very subtle and destructive. It is so subtle that we are usually totally unaware of what we are doing. To us it is perfectly clear that the fault lies not in ourselves, but in the other, whether our next-door neighbour or the Russians. The habit is destructive, because it harms our neighbour, whether an individual or a nation, but leaves the real cause of the destruction untouched, precisely because we have refused to acknowledge it.

We refuse to acknowledge our own inner chaos because we are all afraid of rejection. Rejection of ourselves by some people is tolerable, as long as there are some others who will still support and assure us that we matter. What we fear most of all is total rejection, launching us into the abyss of self-rejection, into nothingness and meaninglessness. If we can face that fear we can reach the truth of ourselves, namely that we have no meaning of ourselves because we are essentially related creatures, that there is no 'I' independently of my relationship to other human beings and with all creation. This web of relationships in which we live is neither an abstraction, nor a complex of blind, irrational forces, but is the unity of God in whom all creation lives and moves and has its being.

The truth of our createdness can appear to us as the truth of our nothingness, and so we fight against it. Anything is preferable to facing this threat, and so we struggle desperately to assure ourselves and to gain assurance from others that we have meaning. We must succeed in some way, must make a mark, must ensure that people notice us. To gain this assurance we may have to pretend that we are other than we really are, feigning a confidence which we do not feel, an interest in things which bore us to death, a liking for people whom we loathe. If we try hard enough we may even convince ourselves that we really are interested in these events, do really care about these people. One pretence leads to another and we are caught up inextricably in a tangled web of deceit. We have become false. We play the game of life without interest, without relish, doing violence to our deepest selves, terrified of criticism and self-questioning. We live among the tombs, and all night and all day among the tombs and in the mountains we howl silently within our souls and do violence to ourselves and to others. Thoreau wrote: 'The mass of men live lives of quiet desperation.'

What I have written will sound exaggerated and unbalanced to some readers who can find no resemblance between themselves and the Gerasene demoniac. Their lives are content, well ordered, virtuous and respectable, and they experience no great frustration, no restless longing, no fear of themselves. This may be because they have already passed through the conflict, have faced their own fears and their pain, have acknowledged their own nothingness without God, in whom they have now found peace; or it may be because they have not yet passed through an emotional infancy and are not yet conscious of what is happening within themselves.

If you are conscious of a similarity between yourself and the Gerasene demoniac, then you have made progress and you are on the track of truth, although it may feel the opposite of progress.

It is true that there is danger in becoming aware of our inner chaos and conflicting desires, which can overpower us and lead us to do what we do not want to do. If, like the Gerasene demoniac, we can take ourselves to Christ and show him the mess we are in, then provided we keep the focus on him as we show him our own problems, he does begin to illuminate our inner darkness, revealing to us desires which we did not know were in us and which go beyond anything we had thought or imagined, even in our wildest dreams. It is the power of these deeper desires which can overcome, subdue and bring into order and harmony those other desires which had been tearing us apart. In other words, the answer to the conflict that is in us is to turn to God, or, for Christians who believe that Jesus is the image of the God we cannot see, turn to Jesus. But what does it mean, 'turn to God' or 'turn to Jesus'? Can I be sure that there is a God? Even if I believe there is a God, can I be sure it is God to whom I am turning and not some private image of my own, a projection of myself, whom I call God?

When I was teaching at Stonyhurst, besides the atheist class of 15-year-olds, I also taught religion to a very bright class of 13-year-olds, who were forever asking for a proof that God exists. St Thomas Aquinas's 'Five Ways', St Anselm's ontological argument, and any others I could find, which had satisfied the great minds of old, failed to impress this class; and they made the very valid point that if they were not sure of God's existence, then what was the point in having two religion periods every week, not to mention daily Mass and other religious services? That God should be accepted as a working hypothesis until the end of term did not satisfy them.

If we insist that we must first prove that God exists before we turn to him, then we shall never find him, because we are trying to treat the God of our being as though he were an intellectual problem which we can solve, define clearly, put in his place and then grant him what we consider his due. Such a God does not exist. We may, by intellectual argument, reach the conclusion, 'Therefore, there must be an uncaused cause' or 'Therefore, there must be a necessary being, and to the uncaused cause and necessary being we shall give the name "God",' but such an intellectual conclusion, although it may be a useful step, does not bring us to a personal God, to the God of Abraham, Isaac and Jacob and to the Father of Our Lord Jesus Christ. The God of the philosophers and the God of the Old Testament prophets are very different Gods. The God of the prophets is mysterious but he is also full of feeling, a God of great compassion, tenderness and love, and therefore also of anger, wrath and fury when those he loves and cherishes treat one another unjustly. The God of the philosophers is remote and impersonal: the God of the prophets is like a two-edged sword which pierces our inner life, laying bare our inner thoughts and feelings, the most base as well as the most sublime, and the psalms are full of both.

The ancient writers of the Church said of prayer that it is 'Heart speaking to heart'. We find God, the true, living and loving God, first with our hearts, and only then can we also find him with our minds. It is not that our hearts are mindless. The heart has its reasons, but they are often hidden from our conscious minds which only catch up with the reasons later.

In turning to God we must first acknowledge that whatever and however he is, he is mystery. We can never, with our finite minds, adequately grasp who he is. If you are searching for a clear and precise notion of who God is, you will not find him in reading this book, and if ever you do find a neat and clear definition, you may be sure that it is false. God is mystery: but that does not mean he is totally unintelligible. We can come to know a mystery and grow in knowledge of it, but the more we enter into the mystery of God, or more accurately, the more the mystery of God takes hold on us, the more we realize that he is mystery.

This truth about God, that he is mystery, is of fundamental importance. Being fundamental, any religion which ignores this truth will certainly lead us astray. We may construct a most elaborate and ingenious religious system, but if it is not grounded in this basic truth that God is mystery, then our elaborate system becomes an elaborate form of idolatry. We are constantly tempted to make God in our own image and likeness. We want to control and domesticate him, giving him perhaps a position of great honour in our hearts, home and country, but we remain in control. God is uncontrollable, beyond anything we can think or imagine. 'God', I once heard someone say, 'is a beckoning word.' He calls us out of ourselves and beyond ourselves, he is the God of surprises, always creating anew. That is why a Church which is static and immutable in its ways cannot be a sign, an effective sign, of his presence in the world. Because we want to control God, there will always be a following for any church which presents God in very clear terms and offers an access card to him, procurable by following the clear prescriptions of that Church. Any deviation from these prescriptions will be presented as deviation from God himself.

When the Second Vatican Council began in 1962, the first draft document considered was 'The Constitution on the Church'. The draft so emphasized the institutional element that its opening chapter was on the hierarchical structure of the Church. The bishops rejected this draft. The first chapter of the final version is entitled 'The Mystery of the Church'. This was a most important beginning, which set the tone for the remainder of the Council and accounts for the great changes which have taken place in the Catholic Church since the Council, and will continue to take place.

The Church is 'the sacrament of God's presence' in the world. Some Christian denominations might object to the word 'sacrament', but most would agree that the Church is a sign, and an effective sign, of God's presence amongst us. God is not static. The Church, if she is to be true to her meaning, cannot be static. We can never adequately describe God: therefore, we can never adequately describe the meaning and nature of the Church. As an organization of human beings, the Church must have structures, laws, discipline, a body of teaching and ways of communicating, but its structures are provisional and it must constantly be developing. God is always greater, greater than his Church. He is at work in all his creation and dwells within each one. As the Book of Wisdom puts it:

> Yes, you love all that exists, you hold nothing of what you have made in abhorrence, for had you hated anything, you would not have made it. And how, had you not willed it, could a thing persist, how be conserved if not called forth by you? You spare all things because all things are yours, Lord, lover of life, you whose imperishable spirit is in all. (Wisd. 11:25–7)

He is at work in the heart of every human being, loves each one and is drawing each to himself. He is no respecter of persons or of our human hierarchies of rank and status, which he upsets: 'He casts the mighty from their thrones and raises the lowly.' He is at work across the Christian denominations, across the religions and in the hearts of those who profess to have no religion. No religion can monopolize God, although most of them will try to do so, claiming that unless you follow their particular way, you cannot be saved.

We are constantly tempted to make God in our own image, to divinize our narrowness and self-importance and then call it the will of God. God is mystery, a beckoning word, and he calls us out beyond our narrowness. Our one security is that he *is*, not in our formulation of how he is.

Because we are made in God's image, therefore we share in his mystery. If we all have different finger-prints, it is not so surprising that we should also have our own unique way of knowing and understanding God. We are all making the same journey, but the route is different for each and we have to discover it in freedom. There are guidelines given to us within the Christian Church through Scripture above all, and through the teaching tradition of the Church, but ultimately we must find our own way and we are responsible for our own journey.

God is the destination of our journey, but God is mystery, which does not at first seem to be a very helpful piece of information. It is as though someone sends us out on a journey, assures us that the journey is not only necessary, but is a matter of life or death, and when we ask the destination of this all-important journey, they tell us that they do not know, cannot know, but nevertheless wish us 'Bon voyage' and 'Bon courage'.

God is mystery, but if we turn to him, he will lead us. All that we have to do is trust that he will do so. But how do I turn to him with all my being? The general answer to be found in books and from anyone who advises on spiritual matters is, 'Pray to him'. The problem is that having heard this advice and perhaps having read enthusiastic books about the wonderful things that prayer can do and has done for others, when we try to pray we find we are talking to empti-ness, or we become more than ever aware of our inner restless-ness, our inability to concentrate, and we may also discover that we have a deep unwillingness to pray. This reluctance to get started can arise from a variety of reasons, but I shall list a few of the more common.

When we try to pray, we must have some idea of God in our minds, and this idea will influence how we pray and whether we pray. As a university chaplain I used to spend much time listening to people who had either given up their Catholic faith, or were thinking of doing so, or they were worried about their own honesty in continuing as Catholics when they felt that they no longer really believed in the teachings of the Catholic Church. Having listened to them, I always tried to encourage them to speak about their own understanding of God. After many conversations, an identikit image of God formed in my imagination.

God was a family relative, much admired by Mum and Dad, who described him as very loving, a great friend of the family, very powerful and interested in all of us. Eventually we are taken to visit 'Good Old Uncle George'. He lives in a formidable mansion, is bearded, gruff and threatening. We cannot share our parents' professed admiration for this jewel in the family. At the end of the visit, Uncle George turns to address us. 'Now listen, dear,' he begins, looking very severe, 'I want to see you here once a week, and if you fail to come, let me just show you what will happen to you.' He then leads us down to the mansion's basement. It is dark, becomes hotter and hotter as we descend, and we begin to hear unearthly screams. In the basement there are steel doors. Uncle George opens one. 'Now look in there, dear,' he says. We see a nightmare vision, an array of blazing furnaces with little demons in attendance, who hurl into the blaze those men, women and children who failed to visit Uncle George or to act in a way he approved. 'And if you don't visit me, dear, that is where you will most certainly go', says Uncle George. He then takes us upstairs again to meet Mum and Dad. As we go home, tightly clutching Dad with one hand and Mum with the other, Mum leans over us and says, 'And now don't you love Uncle George with all your heart and soul, mind and strength?' And we, loathing the monster, say, 'Yes I do,' because to say anything else would be to join the queue at the furnace. At a tender age religious schizophrenia has set in and we keep telling Uncle George how much we love him and how good he is and that we want to do only what pleases him. We observe what we are told are his wishes and dare not admit, even to ourselves, that we loathe him.

Uncle George is a caricature, but a caricature of a truth, the truth that we can construct a God who is an image of our tyrannical selves. Hell-fire sermons are out of fashion, but they were in fashion a few decades ago and they may well come in again. Such sermons have a great appeal to certain unhealthy types of mind, but they cause havoc with the more healthy and sensitive.

Our notion of God is mediated to us through parents, teachers and clergy. We do not come to know God directly. If our experience of parents and teachers has been of dominating people who show little affection or respect for us as persons, but value us only in so far as we conform to their expectations, then this experience is bound to affect our notion of God and will influence the way we relate to him. Our notion of God is not only inadequate; it may also be distorted. Intellectually, I may know that God is not like Uncle George, but it is my feelings about God which determine how I approach him, and they do not change as easily as my ideas. Uncle George is not easily exorcised from my emotions and, although I may know in my mind that God is not like that, I may still experience a strong disinclination to approach him, without knowing why, and find a thousand reasons for not praying – I am too busy, I prefer to find him through my work, etc. We have to pray constantly to be rid of false notions of God, and we have to beg him to teach us who he is, for no one else can. 'God is known by God alone,' as one of the early writers of the Church said. What we are praying for is not merely an intellectual knowledge, but a felt knowledge which affects our whole being and therefore affects the way we see ourselves, other people and the world around us. This felt knowledge of God changes the patterns of our thinking and therefore of acting, breaks open the cocoon of our minds and hearts and liberates us from the constrictions which our upbringing and present environment are imposing on us.

Uncle George is one caricature of a false notion of God, but there are many others. We may get rid of Uncle George and put in his place a Santa Claus notion of God, a benevolent figure who enters our life occasionally to give us presents. He is nice to have around as long as everything is going well, but when disaster strikes we give up believing in him. Santa Claus is closer to God, who is love, than Uncle George, but bears little relation to the God of Scripture who 'counts the very hairs of our heads' and who 'created my inmost self and put me together in my mother's womb'.

The particular image we have of God will depend very much on the nature of our upbringing and how we have reacted to it, because our ideas and our felt knowledge derive from our experience. If our experience has taught us to think of God as a policemanlike figure, whose predominant interest is in our faults, and if our encounters with him have been mostly in cold churches where we were bored out of our minds with barely audible services and sermons presenting God as he who disapproves of most of the things we like, then we are not likely to want to turn to him, no matter how many people may tell us that prayer is necessary.

To become aware that we have a distorted notion of God is to have made progress on our journey towards him. As the journey continues, we shall discover other distortions of which we were not aware. Such discoveries can be very painful at first, but it is like the pain we feel when our limbs are at last free after being constricted; it is the pain of freedom. The journey to God is a journey of discovery and it is full of surprises. Here is an example of someone who discovered, through prayer, his own distorted notion of God.

'Fred' was considered a model Christian. He was young, married and, in addition to his professional work, he belonged to several voluntary bodies, took an intelligent interest in theology, lived a very simple life-style, rarely dining out or going to films or theatre, and he and his wife spent most of their holiday time at conferences. On one of his holidays he came to make an individually given retreat. I encouraged him to pray by using his imagination on scenes from the Gospel, entering the scene as though it were now happening and himself a participant. At the end of each day he would tell me what he had experienced in these scenes. One day he had been imagining the marriage feast at Cana. He had a vivid imagination and had seen tables heaped with food set out beneath a blue sky. The guests were dancing and it was a scene of great merriment. 'Did you see Christ?' I asked. 'Yes,' he said, 'Christ was sitting upright on a straight-backed chair, clothed in a white robe, a staff in his hand, a crown of thorns on his head, looking disapproving.'

The imagination is a wonderful and much neglected faculty. It enables us to enter into the scenes of the Gospel with our senses and our feelings as well as with our minds, but it also projects into our conscious minds thoughts, memories and feelings which, although hidden from us in our subconscious, are, in fact, influencing our perception, thinking and acting. In Fred's case this image of Christ revealed much to him about his basic image of God and of Christ which had been hidden from him earlier. Before praying this Cana scene, if he had been asked, 'What is your basic notion of God and of Christ?', he would probably have answered, 'God is the God of love, mercy and compassion.' Deep down in his subconscious another image of God was effectively operating and influencing his life. As he reflected on this image of the disapproving Christ, he began to understand many things in his own life. He saw a Christ who disapproved of merriment, who demanded an unceasing application to 'good works', a tyrannical Christ who did not permit the simple pleasures of life. He began to realize that he had never allowed himself to admit the truth that he really experienced no joy in his multiple commitments to good works. He felt constantly guilty and driven by an inexorable God. The more he was advised, and advised himself, to turn to God and pray, the worse he felt, but the 'oughts' in his life were so strong that he could not refuse to pray. He was suffering from what the late Dr Frank Lake, author of *Clinical Theology*, used to call 'a hardening of the oughteries'.

This discovery was very painful for Fred at first, but it was the beginning of his release from a tyrannical image of God. Fred's past life had not been a waste. He had sincerely followed God as he knew him, and this sincere following brought him to a new road. God was teaching him through his imagination and through his feelings.

I often shudder when I hear, or read, the advice 'pray and all will be well', for I have met too many people who have been broken by this kind of advice to be able to give it glibly. If a false and tyrannical God is operating in the person, then what I am saying is 'return to your tyrant'.

Freud invented the term 'super-ego'. Briefly, it refers to that part of our mind, conscious and subconscious, which has so assimilated the 'oughts' of childhood, given to us by parents and others, that the 'oughts' have become a permanent part of our thinking and are accepted as our own decision. Take, for example, the child for whom its parents have great hopes and they are constantly urging the child to do better. 'Only the best is good enough for our family,' perhaps reinforced with, 'only the best is good enough for God.' The child struggles and fails, but failure is intolerable because it incurs the wrath of Mum and Dad, and, if God has been introduced, his wrath too descends on the child. The child, like any child, has a desperate need of affection and security, which are as important for its survival as food and shelter. The child struggles on. Winning Mum's approval becomes the object of its existence. Eventually, if Mum is strong enough and the child is too weak to enter the critical stage of its development, it will become a model child in Mum's eyes. She will revel in the child's success, docility and regard for her. The child will assimilate to itself mother's ambitions, and, long after mother's death, her ambition will remain goading the child on throughout its life. The child's own personality has never had a chance to grow and so it will live a driven, frustrated, anxious life, but without knowing the reason. The reason is that the child's own ego has never had the chance to grow. It will never find freedom until liberated from this tyrannical super-ego. Without that liberation the child, now an adult, will live striving to attain an ideal which tortures and wears out both physically and mentally, because the ideal is alien to it.

In Christianity, emphasis on the institutional element, especially if it includes a heavy dose of moral teaching imposed with threats of eternal damnation for non-observance and excludes the critical and mystical, can have the same effect on its members as the ambitious mother on her child. Christianity imposed in this way will develop a tyrannical religious super-ego in its members, stifling the individual personality, depriving them of inner freedom and leading them into a state of Christian neurosis. Christ's yoke, instead of being easy and light as he promised, becomes a painful burden which buries us under its weight of anxiety and guilt.

This phenomenon of the super-ego is not something to be found only in psychiatrists' clients. It is in all of us, is a good and necessary element in our growth, especially in infancy, but if we are to develop as human beings, we have to learn to shed the super-ego. We cannot love and serve God with all our heart and mind and soul and strength if we have not yet found a mind and heart of our own.

Our treasure lies hidden in the field of our own experience and in the inner life which results from that experience. In this chapter we have looked a little more closely at the complexity of our inner life with its conflicting desires and emotions. Our temptation is to ignore this inner life, but it refuses to be ignored. If not acknowledged and harmonized, it will, sooner or later, take us by surprise, sometimes in ways which can harm both ourselves and others. Spiritual writers tell us to turn to God in prayer, but God, for us, can become part of the complexity. False images of God operating within us can make us more fearful, exercising a ruthless tyranny which stifles the life in us. In the following chapter I shall suggest some methods of prayer which can enable us to detect more quickly any false images of God which may be operating.

Exercise

Read St Mark's Gospel 5:1–20 slowly, pondering the description which Mark gives of the demoniac. Scribble down any personal experience which comes to mind as you read this description. Finally, imagine yourself standing on the edge of the cliff with Jesus and, as the pigs drop into the lake, hear him say to you, 'There goes your gloom, there goes your anger, your bitterness, your hate, etc.'

4

Tools for Digging – Some Methods of Prayer

Be still and know that I am God. (Psalm 46:10)

This chapter suggests some methods of prayer. They are suggestions, not prescriptions, and describe only a few methods. If you do not find them helpful, it does not follow that you cannot pray, but only that you do not find these methods helpful. There are as many ways of praying as there are human beings. Everyone has the ability to pray and each must find their own way. The suggestions in this chapter are simply a few methods which may help the reader to get started, for that is all you need to do. I have belaboured this point because it is of fundamental importance. God alone can teach us how to pray. We must not allow particular methods to get in the way.

In ancient times peoples could be enslaved by wicked kings, cruel tyrants and sadistic emperors. In modern times, in democratic as well as in totalitarian countries, we are enslaved by experts, who can, if we allow them, control every detail of our lives. Fortunately, the experts rarely agree among themselves. If, for example, the medical profession were always unanimous in the assertions of their experts, there would be little left which we could safely eat or drink and few forms of exercise which we could safely perform. Experts in psychology and psychiatry can become an even greater threat to our freedom, if we have such an exaggerated respect for their views that we assume our own thoughts and instinctive feelings on any subject must be mistaken. They can then dictate to us how children should be reared and how we are to think, feel and act if we are to become integrated, meaningful, humane, beautiful persons. Totalitarian governments recognize the value of control by the expert and so they label their recalcitrant dissidents 'psychiatric patients' and send them off for treatment.

The Roman emperors did not need psychologists and psychiatrists to help them control dissidents. Their pagan subjects were religious people who believed in gods, so the emperors declared themselves to be divine and so hoped to gain a more complete control over the minds and hearts of their subjects, not all of whom could be controlled by the provision of bread and circuses. Christ was tempted to exercise the same kind of control, to turn stones into bread, to put on a show by leaping from the temple, and finally to take over all the kingdoms of the world. He rejected all these temptations: 'You must worship the Lord your God and serve him alone.' Religious authorities and teachers will always be tempted to control and dominate in the name of God. Christ warned his followers against submitting to this kind of domination:

> You must not allow yourselves to be called Rabbi, since you have only one Master, and you are all brothers. You must call no one on earth your father, since you have only one Father, and he is in heaven. Nor must you allow yourselves to be called teachers, for you have only one Teacher, the Christ. (Matt. 23:9–11)

We need doctors, psychiatrists, religious teachers and specialists in every branch of knowledge, and we should be fools if we did not listen to them, but we must never allow any expert to dominate our lives. We need religious teachers and authorities, and we need an institutional element in the Church which includes authoritative teaching, but the object of all Christian teaching and of all the discipline and laws within the Church is to make us more perceptive, responsive and obedient to God at work within us. If the mystical element is not emphasized in the Church and if we do not meet God within our own unique inner selves, our religion can degenerate into an idolatry of the institution, or the worship of an ideology, a system of ideas.

God really is our teacher and he alone can teach us to pray, or rather, he alone prays in us. 'The spirit you received', St Paul tells the Romans, 'is not the spirit of slaves bringing fear into your lives again; it is the spirit of sons, and it makes us cry out, 'Abba, Father' (Rom. 8:14–15). If, in prayer, you find yourself constantly asking yourself, 'Am I praying the right way?', that is an indication that you are allowing yourself to be controlled and dominated by other peoples' suggestions. God wants to share with you in the unique being he has given you: he does not want you to approach him as though he can only respond to set formulae prescribed for us by those who know. We have to learn to trust our own experience, our richest source of knowledge. We must listen to others who can help us read and interpret our own experience, but we must not allow them so to dominate our thinking that we ignore our own inner promptings, for to do so is to renounce our freedom and 'to lose our very selves'.

Many people cannot get started on prayer because they are doubtful about their own faith in God, or because they feel their lives are in such a mess that they cannot possibly approach God until they have reformed. If you are so affected, it is good to ask, 'What are the basic assumptions underlying my disinclination to pray?' Am I assuming that my subjective state of uncertain belief is all important, or that my failures are greater than God's goodness? To begin prayer it is sufficient to acknowledge that I am not self-sufficient, that I am not the creator of myself and of creation. If I can do this, then I acknowledge that there is some power – I may not know whether it is personal or not and may be in complete ignorance of its nature – greater than I.

Prayer is a listening. The psalmist says: 'Be still, and know that I am God.' It is difficult to be still, even physically still, but even more difficult to be still in our minds. The more we try to quieten our minds, the more our thoughts and memories begin to buzz around like a swarm of angry bees. One of the greatest obstacles in prayer is the activity of our minds which send up such a barrage of thoughts, memories and ideas that God, whose ways are not our ways and whose thoughts are not our thoughts, is not allowed entry. We are like cocooned creatures, the hard outer covering representing our narrow vision of ourselves and of the world. When we pray with busy minds it is as though we rattle the cocoon while remaining within it: when we are still the cocoon can begin to open.

Fortunately, our minds are so constructed that normally

we can only concentrate on one thing at a time. If I can concentrate all my attention on what I am feeling in my big toe, I cannot worry about my finances at the same time, so here is one suggestion for practising stillness of mind and body.

Sit in a straight-backed chair, or if you are agile enough, in the lotus position or crossed-legged on the floor, your back straight without being rigid, the body relaxed, your feet, if you are on a chair, planted firmly on the ground and your hands at rest on your thighs or joined in your lap. Close your eyes, or fix them on some point in front of you. Now let your whole attention focus on what you can feel in your body. You may start at your feet and work upwards, letting your attention dwell, perhaps only for a few seconds, on whatever part of the body you can feel, shifting attention from one part to the other, although the longer you can hold attention on one part, the better. Your attention is on what you are feeling, not on thoughts about feeling. If you are uncomfortable, or itch and want to move position, just acknowledge the discomfort, assure yourself that it is all right and, without moving, continue to focus attention on what you can feel in the body. The mind rarely leaves us long in peace to do this, but begins to demand attention with comment and questions. 'This is a waste of valuable time. What has this to do with prayer? Is this some kind of Hindu thing? What is the point of it?' Deal with the questions and comment as you dealt with the itch; acknowledge the comments and questions, then return to feeling the body. It may be enough to attempt this exercise for five minutes at a time at first, then try to lengthen the period. You will begin to know how difficult it is to keep the mind still and quiet but, with gentle persistence, concentration improves and you will feel the relaxing effect of it. Many people find that this exercise makes them very drowsy and it can be a useful exercise for insomniacs!

Having done this exercise and experienced some degree of stillness, you can, if you like, move into more explicit prayer by repeating to yourself St Paul's phrase, which he borrowed from the Stoics. 'In him I live, and move, and have my being.' In every experience of our lives we encounter God. The more we are in touch with ourselves, the more we are in touch with him. As you pray in this way, avoid, as far as you can, any self-judgement, whether of approval or disapproval, because it is in these judgements that our false notions of God are likely to be most operative. If you cannot avoid self-judgement, then treat the judgement as you treated the itch: acknowledge its presence, but turn your attention back to your feelings.

Another similar exercise is to sit in the same position as already described, this time concentrating all your attention on the physical feelings of breathing in and breathing out, without deliberately changing the rhythm of your breathing. Focus attention on feeling the cold air entering your nostrils and the warm air when you exhale. At first you may become self-conscious about your breathing and find it becomes irregular, but this does not, as a rule, continue. If it were to do so and you find yourself becoming breathless, then this exercise is not for you at present. Most people find that on doing this exercise the pattern of their breathing changes, the breath becoming deeper and slower, and they begin to feel drowsy. In itself, it is a very good relaxation exercise, but if you care to use it for more explicit prayer, then let the in-breathing express all that you long for in life, however impossible it may seem in practice, and let the out-breath express your surrender of everything to God, all of your life with its worries, sins, guilt and regrets. Again, it is very important to do this without self-judgement, whether of approval or disapproval. Keep your attention fixed on your desire to hand over all these worries about self and do not clutch at them as if they were a treasured possession.

These suggestions for finding stillness must be accepted for what they are, namely suggestions, not imperatives. What is imperative is that you should eventually find stillness in prayer, but how you do it is going to vary with each person. Some people can only get to sleep by lying very still: others can only do so if they roll restlessly from side to side for a while. Some find stillness by sitting: others may have to walk about first. To busy, active people these stillness exercises can appear to be a waste of time. The more active and busy we are, the more necessary and helpful the stillness.

Another very simple form of prayer following on a stillness exercise is to pray through our own body, offering each limb and each sense to God and asking him to channel his goodness through every particle of our being. In a poem 'The Blessed Virgin compared to the Air we Breathe', Gerard Manley Hopkins says of Mary that she

> This one work has to do –
> Let all God's glory through.

We speak of a 'glorious dawn' when the rising sun dispels the night, and what was dark and formless is revealed in all its beauty. We cannot see the glory of God in itself, but only in its effects upon creation, so we pray that his glory may be manifested through his action on creation and, in particular, that the glory of his goodness may be channelled through the work of our hands, his tenderness and compassion through our eyes, his life and peace-giving power through our lips, etc.

Christian tradition recognizes that it is difficult for busy and active people to be still, and that is why many traditional methods of prayer are very repetitive, the repetition being designed to still the mind. If the repetition is also rhythmic, either in time with our step if we are walking, or with our breathing if we are physically still, it can be even more effective. The repetition may be of a single word, or of a simple phrase, like the famous pilgrim prayer, 'Lord Jesus Christ have mercy on me', or of a longer prayer, for example, the Our Father, each syllable being repeated in time with our step if we are walking, or with our breath if physically still. Many traditional forms of prayer began as pilgrim prayers. When walking it is more difficult to concentrate the mind than when we are still, but the constant repetition of a word or phrase in time with our step can induce an inner stillness of mind. In such a stillness, the rhythmic repetition may cease. If this happens, let it happen and do not continue with the rhythmic repetition. In general, follow your own inner promptings in prayer rather than be slavishly obedient to some prescribed method.

Psalm 131 describes a basic disposition which should permeate all our prayer, a childlike trust in God:

> Yahweh, my heart has no lofty ambitions,
>   my eyes do not look too high.
> I am not concerned with great affairs

or marvels beyond my scope.
Enough for me to keep my soul tranquil and quiet
    like a child in its mother's arms,
as content as a child that has been weaned.
Israel, rely on Yahweh,
    now and for always!

God is in all things. God is within my own being, constantly creating it. The object of all prayer methods is to help us to meet God 'closer to me than I am to myself'. For Christians, the primary source for prayer is in the Bible, a collection of very diverse writings accepted by the Church as 'inspired'. Volumes have been written on the meaning of 'inspiration'. Briefly, we can accept it as meaning that by reading, pondering and praying from these writings we are listening to God speaking to us now. The word of God in Scripture is a special sacrament of his presence, just as real, although different in form, as his presence in the Eucharist. The words of Scripture, if we read them with faith, act like a light falling on the darkness of our inner selves so that we can find and recognize that God – Father of Abraham, Isaac and Jacob, and Father of Our Lord Jesus Christ – is also our God. I read and ponder God's action in past ages in order to recognize that same action continuing now in me. In the remainder of this chapter I shall suggest some ways of praying from the Scriptures.

In praying from the Scriptures, choose a passage which in some way appeals to you. If you are a beginner at this kind of prayer, have a brief look at some of the psalms, or at a few passages from the prophets, or at some of the New Testament epistles until you find some passage, or phrase which attracts you. (A few passages are given at the end of this chapter.) To illustrate the method, I shall take a passage from Isaiah, originally spoken by the prophet to the captive Israelites, exiled, hopeless, without any prospect of returning to their own land. The passage is included in the Scriptures not primarily as a piece of historical information, nor as a fine example of Hebrew poetry, but because it expresses the mind and heart of God for all people and for all time, so that when I read these words I hear God addressing me at this moment. It can be helpful to begin the prayer by spending a few

46

moments pondering the mystery of our own being. Our body is a most complex structure containing, literally, billions of cells, each most mysterious and intricate in form, yet all interconnected and unified in a wonderful harmony, an internal communications system which makes all the world's transport systems seem clumsy in comparison. The billions of cells which form me are co-ordinated and linked with every other particle in the universe, as though the whole universe is itself one giant organism. No man is an island. When a baby throws its rattle out of its pram, the heavens rock. When I read the Scriptures, it is good to hear the words as if they were coming not from a page of print outside me, but as if they were words coming from within the mystery of my own being. In this way we can listen to Isaiah:

> But now, thus says Yahweh, who created you, Jacob, who formed you, Israel: Do not be afraid, for I have redeemed you; I have called you by your name, you are mine. Should you pass through the sea, I will be with you; or through rivers, they will not swallow you up. Should you walk through fire, you will not be scorched and the flames will not burn you. For I am Yahweh, your God, the Holy One of Israel, your saviour. . . . Because you are precious in my eyes, because you are honoured and I love you, I give men in exchange for you, peoples in return for your life. Do not be afraid, for I am with you. (Isa. 43:1–5)

Read over the passage several times and see if any word or phrase stands out for you, and stay with that phrase for as long as you like before turning your attention to any other. The process is analogous to sucking a boiled sweet. Do not try to analyse the phrase just as you would not normally break up a boiled sweet and subject it to chemical analysis before tasting. Often a phrase will catch the attention of our subconscious mind's needs long before our conscious mind is aware of the reason for the attraction. That is why it is good to remain with the phrase for as long as possible without trying to analyse it.

Let us suppose that the phrase which stands out is 'Don't be afraid, for I have redeemed you'. Having stayed with the phrase for a few seconds, it may well happen that the mind then begins to fill with questions and apparent distractions.

'How do I know that I am not deceiving myself? How do I know these words are true, that God really does communicate himself through them? Do I really have faith in God?' These are valid questions, but let them wait for the time being, for if we begin to tangle with them at the beginning of the prayer we shall never get started. 'Unless you become as little children, you cannot enter the kingdom of heaven.' Our questionings are like an artillery barrage which keeps God away from our hearts. If we can begin to let his words into our heart and feelings, then we may begin to see our questions differently.

When a child is frightened in the night, mother goes and lifts the child and says, 'It's all right,' and the child gradually quietens. But if she has a prodigy on her hands who replies, 'But mother, what epistemological and metaphysical assumptions are you making in that statement and what empirical evidence can you adduce in support of your contention?' then mother really has a problem in her arms. In prayer we act like that impossible child if we refuse to listen to God until he has measured up to whatever criteria we may care to lay down. We communicate with him first with our hearts. The heart is not mindless: it has its reasons, deeper than we can see at first with our conscious minds.

Having left the questions aside for the time being, what do I do with all the other distractions which flood my mind? I may begin to wonder whether I turned the gas off, or remember a letter I forgot to post, or a phone call I should have made. If the distraction is urgent, like the gas, the safest thing is to go and check. With other matters that can wait, perhaps jot them down on a piece of paper to be attended to later. Any other matters which come to mind, far from being distractions, can become the substance of my prayer. It is as though the phrase of Scripture is a searchlight which plays upon my stream of consciousness, thoughts, memories, reflections, daydreams, hopes, ambitions, fears, and I pray out of the mixture of God's word and my inner thoughts and feelings. The opening verse of the Bible, 'Now the earth was a formless void, there was darkness over the deep, and God's spirit hovered over the water,' is describing a present state of affairs, not a past event, and when I pray from the Scriptures

I am letting the spirit of God hover over the chaos and darkness of my being.

When I allow the word of God to hover over my preoccupations, then anything can happen, for he is the God of surprises. It is important that I do not hide my inner chaos from the word of God or from myself. I may, for example, having fastened on the phrase 'Do not be afraid, for I have redeemed you', feel my own fears arising, fear of my own inadequacy, or health, or sinful tendencies, or of other people who are a threat to me. I may then begin to feel angry at these soothing words of Isaiah, which, far from allaying my fears are simply intensifying them. The words seem hollow and I feel anger with God, or find myself confronted with my own disbelief, and think there is no point in continuing. The spirit of God is hovering over my chaos and it is important that I allow it to do so, so that the Spirit may produce life and order out of my chaos. We are often so trained that we think it wrong to allow any negative feelings entry into our prayer, especially negative feelings about God. We have to learn to grow out of this training, expressing our feelings and thoughts freely before God and trusting that he is big enough to take our tantrums. It is only when we are free to express our negative feelings that we can reach deeper feelings in us of tenderness and compassion. God is in truth, never in pretence. There is no point in pretending in prayer before God, who knows us better than we know ourselves.

To sum up this method of praying from the Scriptures in a sentence: Choose a passage of Scripture, read it over several times, focus your attention on any phrase which appeals to you, let this phrase hover over whatever comes to your mind and then speak to God as simply and honestly as you can, knowing that he loves the chaos that is you and that his Spirit working in you can do infinitely more than you can think or imagine.

There is no thought, feeling or desire within us which cannot become the substance of our prayer. 'Distractions' do not refer to thoughts and feelings, but to the direction of our attention. For example, I may in prayer remember a crossword clue and find myself trying to find the word. I can turn this searching into prayer, 'Lord, keep me searching for the one clue that matters, the clue to my emptiness and longings, the clue to the meaning of my life.' The crossword clue is no longer a distraction, but has become a springboard to prayer. It is only a distraction if I allow it so to preoccupy me that I turn my attention away from prayer altogether and search for an ten-letter word for 'inattentive while being pulled apart'.

I have already made mention of the use of the imagination in prayer. Imaginative contemplation is especially useful for praying from the Gospels. Read the passage, then imagine the scene as though it were happening at this moment and you were an active participant.

I shall illustrate the method in greater detail with a few verses from St John's Gospel:

> In the evening of that same day, the first day of the week, the doors were closed in the room where the disciples were, for fear of the Jews. Jesus came and stood among them. He said to them, 'Peace be with you', and showed them his hands and his side. The disciples were filled with joy when they saw the Lord, and he said to them again, 'Peace be with you. As the Father sent me, so I am sending you.' (John 20:19–21)

As with any Scripture passage, I approach it believing that through the medium of this passage I can encounter God addressing me at this moment. In this passage I meet the Risen Christ, Lord of all creation, offering me his peace. For the moment I lay aside my intellectual questioning and doubts about my own faith – did the resurrection really happen? what is its nature? what certainty can I have? why are the resurrection narratives so conflicting and sometimes contradictory? is there not a danger that I am simply fooling myself by using this method of prayer? might I not end up some kind of religious fanatic if I pray in this way? These are all valid questions: to lay them aside for the moment is not to run away from them, for they can be considered later. But if I insist on trying to answer them before I begin to pray imaginatively, I shall never get started.

I try to imagine the scene as St John depicts it. The immediate reaction of many people to this suggestion is, 'But I have no imagination', meaning usually, 'I am not a creative or artistic type of person'. If you are capable of recalling even one event of your past life and reliving it in memory, however blurred the details, then you have the ability to pray imaginatively. I have met many people who are unwilling to try this method, but I have never met anyone incapable of using their imagination. Peoples' imaginative ability varies. Some can imagine with clear pictorial detail and are able to see the size and furnishings of the room, the colour of the walls, the nature of the lighting, the expressions on the disciples' faces, etc., while others will not see any of these details, the picture being very blurred and indefinite. The details are not important. What is important is that, through the use of our imagination, we should come to know the reality of the Risen Jesus, as real today as on the day of his resurrection, entering into the closed room of my inner fears and still saying to me, 'Peace be to you,' and showing me his hands and his side.

There should be nothing hurried in this or in any other form of prayer. It may take quite a long time to let the scene build up. Talk in imagination to the characters in the scene, listening to them and telling them about your own fears. Sometimes, when praying from this passage, people can enter the upper room without much difficulty, can sense the fear in the disciples and become more conscious of their own, but as soon as they reach 'Jesus came and stood among them. He said to them "Peace be with you" ', they go blank and the scene disappears, or they feel excluded from it, as though the scene is happening elsewhere and they are insulated from it.

They then conclude that their prayer is a failure and abandon it. It has not failed, for imagination is revealing an aspect of their own reality, and it is important to stay with the scene and keep praying to Christ from wherever our imagination may take us. Just as in the previous method of praying from Scripture we saw that what are termed 'distractions' can become the substance of our prayer, so here the meanderings of the imagination can form the subject matter of the prayer. If, for example, I go blank as soon as Christ enters and I cannot see him, or hear him say to me 'Peace', this may be revealing my tendency to keep him out of my mind and heart, to hide my own fears even from myself, to keep the doors of my own inner life firmly shut, letting Christ in only when I decide. The imagination is revealing deep layers of consciousness which are closed to the Risen Christ and to the peace which he gives. The prayer is revealing to me my need for his peace and so I can now pray to him from a deeper level of my being.

In general, in this method of prayer let imagination lead, but keep the focus of your attention on Christ, so that the imagining does not degenerate into a Walter Mitty type of fantasy, in which the focus of attention becomes yourself, whether relishing your imagined heroism or deploring your imagined wickedness. Even if this were to happen, it can still be a revealing prayer, showing a tendency to take over from Christ and to make ourselves the centre of everything. One person in contemplating the upper room found himself trying to soothe the fears and cheer up the depressed and frightened apostles, doing it so successfully that he felt resentment when Christ appeared and said, 'Peace be with you'. This was a shattering experience for the man, because he was able to recognize the truth in his own life which his imagination mirrored, a refusal to admit his own fears and his own needs and a tendency to forbid other people to admit theirs, pouring platitudes and dogmatic statements upon them in the name of Christ, whom he had never permitted entry into his own inner self.

Could this method of prayer be dangerous for someone with a very vivid imagination and little emotional stability? It could be dangerous for such a person, especially if practised without constant reference back to Christ, but for the majority of people there is no danger. We have a very tough psychic inner defence system which does not permit entry to memories, feelings or thoughts with which we are unable to cope at the moment. A good general spiritual maxim is, 'Never do violence to yourself'. As long as we observe this and do not force ourselves into an imaginative prayer which we know is likely to overwhelm us, there is little risk of our suffering any harm. The method has been practised from earliest times in the Christian tradition and has inspired generations of Christian artists, poets and spiritual writers.

When Ignatius of Loyola asked for novels during his convalescence and was given instead a copy of Ludolph of Saxony's *Life of Christ*, the book's preface introduced him to this method of imaginative contemplation. Ludolph advised the reader:

Read of what has been done [in the Gospels] as though it were happening now. . . . Offer yourself as present to what was said and done through Our Lord Jesus Christ with the whole affective power of your mind. . . . Hear and see these things being narrated as though you were hearing with your own ears and seeing with your own eyes.

It was this method of imaginative contemplation which started Ignatius on his conversion journey, and his Spiritual Exercises (a carefully graded series of Scripture-based passages designed to allow our hidden self to grow strong) consist mostly of imaginative contemplations.

In our own times, psychologists and psychiatrists have come to appreciate the value and power of our active imagination. Jung used this method to help his clients become more aware of, and open to, the unconscious. St Ignatius was an instinctive psychologist. Modern psychology, especially Jungian, can help us understand and appreciate the value and wisdom in Ignatius' Spiritual Exercises, hidden often in a laconic, abrupt style, an example of which we shall be considering in the next chapter.

In this chapter we have looked at some methods of prayer. In terms of the treasure hidden in the field, it has offered some digging tools. The very important question remains, where do I dig?

A major cause of disillusionment among Christians is the dichotomy we observe in ourselves and others between prayer and action, a dichotomy which Christ observed and castigated so severely: 'Alas for you, scribes and Pharisees, you hypocrites! You who are like whitewashed tombs that look handsome on the outside, but inside are full of dead men's bones and every kind of corruption.' (Matt. 23:27–8)

Why is it that very religious people, who may spend much time in prayer, can often become so intolerant, inhuman and cruel? Their conviction of their own righteousness is so strong that, far from being troubled by their cruelty, they congratulate themselves on their single-minded dedication to the cause of right. They are so convinced that God is on their side, that God's ways and their ways have become indistinguishable. The God of mystery has been reduced and domesticated to become an image of themselves. God is no longer allowed to be God: he is superfluous. This is a temptation which afflicts all of us, the temptation to pride. How are we to avoid this danger of creating God in our own image and likeness? In what direction are we to dig to find the hidden treasure. That is the question we shall be considering in the next chapter.

Exercises

Practise the stillness exercises (pp. 43–4).
Practise the prayer of the senses (pp. 44–5).
Practise some form of rhythmic prayer (p. 45).

For readers not familiar with the Bible, here are a few texts to start with in praying from the Scriptures. (A few texts for imaginative contemplation are given at the end of chapters 7 and 10.)

Psalms 8, 23, 63, 131, 139.
Isaiah 25; 40; 43:1–7; 45:9–13; 54:4–10; 55.
Jeremiah 31:31–4.
Ezekiel 36:22–6.
Hosea 11:1–8.
Wisdom 11:21—12:2.
John 15:1–17.
Romans 8:28–39.
Ephesians 1:3–14; 3:14–21.
Philippians 2:1–11.
Colossians 1:14–20.

5

General Directions for Digging

I lived once in the same house as Fr Patrick Treanor, a Jesuit astronomer, a small man with a large brain and the face of a child. He would often dart out of his room, stop suddenly, spin round several times on his own axis, his finger-tip on his lips, and explain to any passer-by, 'I've forgotten where I'm meant to be going'. Walking with him in the Oxford country-side, especially in spring, was always full of surprises, for he would disappear into a ditch without warning, appearing later gazing in wonder at a wild flower. Having contemplated it, he would then give its genus, species, and point out its particular qualities before disappearing again. He usually arrived home clutching a bouquet. He was never quite sure of his immediate direction, but there was a very clear general direction to his life. He was fascinated by all the wonders of God's creation on earth and in the heavens and this fascination determined the general direction of his life.

When St Ignatius Loyola had written his Spiritual Exercises, he added a short preface, a skeletal summary of the inner journey to be made through his Exercises. Later commentators called this preface 'The First Principle and Foundation'. It may be compared to a small-scale map of a very long journey. Like any small-scale map, it does not look interesting at first sight and gives little detail, but it does give very clear general directions which we shall consider in this chapter. The opening sentence gives the basic direction, and the remaining sentences draw out some of its implications. The preface begins:

Man is created to praise, reverence and serve God, our Lord, and by this means to save his soul.

The essence of this sentence is 'We are created to praise

55

God', because reverence and service and the salvation of our souls follow from praise. This is the fundamental direction. The opposite direction would be to live as though all creation existed to praise, reverence and serve us!

When I was visiting a Centre of Spirituality in the U.S.A. a few years ago, I was met at the station by a Jesuit novice. He led me to a car, turned on the ignition, and when the engine fired he said in a very solemn voice, 'Praise the Lord, thank you, Jesus, thank you,' and off we roared having added our bit to the angelic choirs! When Ignatius says that we are created to praise God, it can hardly mean that we should pepper our prayer, conversation, activity and thinking with the phrase, 'Praise the Lord.'

If you have prepared a meal, do you prefer the guest who keeps exclaiming what a wonderful meal it is, but nibbles and refuses any more, or the guest who demolishes the first plateful like a hungry dog then looks up appealingly for more? Verbal praise is empty flattery if it does not express a genuine appreciation of the object or person praised. This opening sentence is saying, 'You will find the general direction for your journey through life, you will find the treasure hidden in the field, through your appreciation of the world around you.'

We need to ponder and to wonder at this opening sentence. It does not say that we must shun creation, rise above it, despise it, try to separate ourselves from it, but that we should appreciate, value and cherish it. We cannot know God in himself. We can only come to know him through our human experience, through his creation. That is why the early Christian theologians spoke of creation itself as a sacrament, that is, a sign and an effective sign of God's presence.

If I appreciate what is around me, I will also wonder at it, be amazed and astonished by it, feel a kind of reverence for it, especially reverence for the mystery of every human being. Out of appreciation comes praise, and true praise includes reverence and wonder, and the desire to be somehow absorbed and at one with the object of my wonder. This is the root of the desire to serve, the desire to be at one with the harmony of creation, to be taken up in it rather than to try and control it for my own purposes. Gerard Manley Hopkins

describes this fundamental movement of our being which sets
us free from our tyrannical self in one of his black sonnets:

My own heart let me more have pity on; let
Me live to my sad self hereafter kind,
Charitable; not live this tormented mind
With this tormented mind tormenting yet.

I cast for comfort I can no more get
By groping round my comfortless, than blind
Eyes in their dark can day or thirst can find
Thirst's all-in-all in all a world of wet.

Soul, self; come, poor Jackself, I do advise
You, jaded, let be; call off thoughts awhile
Elsewhere; leave comfort root-room; let joy size
At God knows when to God knows what; whose smile
's not wrung, see you; unforeseen times rather – as skies
Betweenpie mountains – lights a lovely mile.

. . . *and by this means to save his soul.* We have emasculated the
word 'soul', thinking of it as an invisible, intangible entity of
which we have no direct experience but which, we are told,
is the most important part of us, being the immortal element
in our being, destined to spend an eternity either in heaven
or in hell. If we think of the soul in this way then we cannot
know what is for its salvation and what leads to its damnation,
because it is invisible and intangible. We must therefore rely
on what other people tell us. We then surrender our freedom
and become slaves to those who can convince us that they
know the vital answers: our own experience becomes an irrel-
evance and we are locked into a religious infantilism.

'Soul' means my very self, the deepest, most sensitive part
of myself, the point of unity in all that I am. The soul manifests itself in everything I experience, whether consciously or
unconsciously. All my longings and hopes, fears and anxieties,
restlessness and ambition are expressions of my soul. There
are many possible ways of describing the phrase 'salvation of
my soul', for example, 'the answer to the indefinable longings
that are in me, to my fear of meaninglessness and inner
emptiness, the answer to my wildest dreams'. In the sonnet
just quoted, Hopkins is describing the pain of his soul locked
in its own thoughts and preoccupations. The escape route

from the prison is through the door of wonder 'as skies betweenpie mountains lights a lovely mile'.

We can compare the soul to a flock of sheep together with the sheep dog. The sheep dog represents the deepest part of the soul, the part St Augustine discovered when he wrote, 'You have created us for yourself, and our hearts are restless until they rest in You' (Confessions, Book 1). The deepest part, the sheep dog, will always be restless until the whole soul is moving towards God. The sheep represent those drives and desires in us which are not integrated into the movement of our being towards God and which keep trying to find satisfaction independently of the deepest part of the soul. We wander this way and that trying to satisfy our hunger, but the deepest part, the sheep dog, keeps harrying us. When we try to satisfy ourselves with something that is not leading us to God, then we feel dissatisfied, bored, empty and frustrated, which is the harrying of the sheep dog. So we try something else and we are harried again. That is why our negative feelings of sadness, anxiety, agitation, etc. can be so important: they can be telling us that our direction is wrong. If we ignore these feelings, or stifle them, we may feel less harried, but we are resting in a false security. It is possible for us so to ignore the harrying of the sheep dog that we no longer notice our negative feelings when we are moving in the wrong direction.

The second sentence of 'The First Principle and Foundation' reads:

The other things on the face of the earth are created for man, to help him in attaining the end for which he is created.

This dry and formal statement is a most optimistic expression of faith, for it is asserting that there is nothing in creation, nothing in our experience, neither the damage done to us nor the damage we have done, no sickness, no weakness physical or mental, which cannot lead us to God. This optimistic statement re-echoes St Paul: 'For I am certain of this: neither life nor death, no angel, no prince, nothing that exists, nothing still to come, not any power, or height or depth, not any created thing, can ever come between us and the love of God made visible in Christ Jesus, our Lord.' (Rom. 8:38–9)

How can the evil done to us, the evil we have done, lead

us to God, for surely these are the very things which separate us from him? The events of our lives may be compared to a ladder stretching from earth to heaven. Some rungs we must grasp firmly and they help us upwards: other rungs we must step on and this also helps us upwards, so the third sentence of 'The Principle and Foundation' reads:

Hence, man is to make use of them [creatures] in so far as they help him in the attainment of his end, and he must rid himself of them in so far as they prove a hindrance to him.

This may sound all very clear and logical, but it has not always been clear in the history of Christian spirituality. There is a constant temptation to despise and reject the limitations of our human nature, and to believe that perfection consists in being as independent of it as possible, a temptation which is at the root of much Christian neurosis.

There are attachments, attitudes and patterns of behaviour, as we saw when considering von Hügel's analysis, which may be helpful and creative at one stage of our life, but may become destructive later. How are we to know what really is helpful and what really is a hindrance? And how am I to rid myself of something which I know to be destructive in my life, if it seems to possess me and I cannot let it go? 'The Principle and Foundation' gives the outline of an answer to these questions in its two final sentences:

Therefore we must make ourselves indifferent to all created things in so far as we are allowed free choice and are not under any prohibition. Consequently, as far as we are concerned, we should not prefer health to sickness, riches to poverty, honour to dishonour, a long life to a short life. The same holds for all other things.

Our one desire and choice should be what is more conducive to the end for which we are created.

Some people take an instant dislike to 'The Principle and Foundation', and, in particular, to these two sentences. If readers share that reaction I can only beg them to suspend judgement at least until the end of this chapter!

Misunderstanding of the meaning of 'indifference' has caused much suffering to individuals and groups within the Christian Church. Lives have been, and still are being, blighted through misunderstanding of the meaning of the word 'indifference', or 'detachment', as though it meant that we are to repress every natural instinct in us for life, health, wealth, reputation, honour, friendship, and that the more we can do so, the more pleasing we are to God. I have known people who have so misunderstood the word 'indifference', thinking that it means repressing every natural inclination, that they have struggled for years to make themselves indifferent in this false sense, encouraged sometimes by their spiritual mentors, until they have reached such a state of detachment from themselves, from other people and from the world around them, and therefore from God, who is in all things, that they have eventually broken down in a state of black despair and experienced hell while still living. What then is the meaning of 'indifference'?

If we are to be free, then we must not be enslaved. If my life is determined and regulated in all its details by my desire for wealth, then I become a slave of the wealth I desire, subordinating every other desire and value of my life to this predominant desire. My relationships to other people will be regulated by my desire for wealth, and my love for truth and justice will also be subordinated to it. Similarly, if I become so enamoured of my own health, or of my power to control others, or of my own self-importance that I subordinate every other desire and value to it, then I am enslaved by these attachments. To be indifferent or detached is the condition of being free. I cannot possibly be free if I repress all my desires and inclinations and feelings, for the more I try to do so, the more I shall be enslaved by them.

I used to look after a black Labrador, called Beuno, from whom I learned much, including a daily illustration of the true meaning of indifference. Every morning I used to collect him from his kennel and take him round to the kitchen door. Once released he leaped around with excitement, trying to move in all directions at once. If he caught the scent of any other human being, he would go after them, returning with a glove or scarf or, on one occasion, with a nun's veil in his mouth; but when I came out of the kitchen with a bone or bacon rinds I would find a transformed Beuno sitting at the entrance, looking as virtuous as his grandfather, a prize-winning gun dog, awaiting his award. He would then follow at heel to my room, ignoring any passers-by, even if they

were carrying gloves, scarves, or wearing veils, and sit motionless save for the saliva streaming from his sad mouth, his eyes
fixed hypnotically on the bone in my hand. At 'heel' he would
come to my side to receive his treasure.

Beuno was a good example of the meaning of indifference.
His attachment to his bone controlled, at least momentarily,
every other desire in him. Indifference, or detachment,
describes the state of a person who is so attached to God that
there is no created thing which they are not ready to let go
if God's will should demand it. To be indifferent does not
mean stifling every desire and inclination, but it does mean
having such an attachment to God and the things of God
that every other attachment is subordinated and in harmony
with it. We can find God only in and through our relationships with other people and with the world around us. We
need to love and be loved, because it is only through these
relationships that we can come to know God, who is Love.
It is through our attachments to other people and to things,
and only through our attachments, that we can find God. We
can no more find God through a complete detachment from
every person and every thing than an express train can find
its destination by being detached from the rails. The indifference and detachment which Ignatius and Christian tradition
teaches is concerned with the direction in which our attachments are leading us. The indifferent person can let go those
attachments which are leading him or her away from God
and change to those which lead more directly to him. That
is why Ignatius ends 'The First Principle and Foundation'
with *Our one desire and choice should be what is more conducive to
the end for which we are created.*

This last sentence of the Preface brings us to the core of the
matter which we are considering in this book. The treasure is
hidden within the field of our own inner life. Our inner life,
which affects the way we perceive the world, act in it and
react to it, is complex, chaotic, a threatening mixture of
thoughts, memories, emotions, desires and fears. The answer
to the chaos is in our desires. 'Trahit sua quemque voluptas,'
wrote the poet Virgil, 'Each is drawn by their own desire';
or expressed more prosaically, 'We all do what we want'.

The problem is the multiplicity and variety of conflicting
desires within us. How are we to discover what we really

desire? Our surface desires are always the most noisy and demanding. When answered, they can leave us feeling empty and sad because in satisfying them we have frustrated deeper desires within us. In the book of Revelation (3:17), the writer tells the unfortunate Church of Laodicea, 'You say to yourself, "I am rich, I have made a fortune, and have everything I want", never realising that you are wretchedly and pitiably poor, and blind and naked too.' This is a realization which often hits men and women in what is called 'the mid-life crisis' and can throw them into depression. In fact, this realization can be the beginning of a new life.

If we were able to discover what we really want, if we could become conscious of the deepest desire within us, then we should have discovered God's will. God's will is not an impersonal blue-print for living forced on us by a capricious God and contrary to almost every inclination in us. God's will is our freedom. He wants us to discover what we really want and who we really are. The struggle is not our will against God's will, but our will struggling with its divided self, the will which wants all creation to praise, reverence and serve me against the will which wants to praise, reverence and serve God, the will which wants to take over from God against the will which wants to let God be God.

The saint is the person who has discovered his/her deepest desire. They then 'do their own thing', which is also God's thing. Their will and God's will are in harmony, so that their lives are characterized by a continuous peace, tranquillity, freedom and joy, even – perhaps especially – in crises and suffering.

If God is not attractive to us, then we cannot desire him. The first step in our journey to him must be to turn towards him and see that he is good beyond all our imagining, that he is 'the joy of man's desiring'. That is why the first message of Christ in the Gospel is 'Repent, and believe the *good* news', and we shall consider this invitation in the next chapter.

Exercises

1. Look again at your obituary notice suggested at the end of chapter 1 and at your faith autobiography suggested

after chapter 2. Do these give you any indication of what you really want?

2. Take a piece of paper and divide it into two columns, the first column headed 'Events which bring me to life' and the second column 'Events which deaden me'. Then look at 'The First Principle and Foundation' again. Does your list give you any indication of the events/attachments which, in your experience, are destructive of life in you and those which are creative?

The full text of 'The First Principle and Foundation' given in this chapter was taken from the Louis J. Puhl edition of the *Spiritual Exercises*, Loyola University Press. Here is my own version, written not as a translation, but as a summary of this chapter:

Before the world was made we were chosen to live in love in God's presence by praising, reverencing and serving him in and through his creation.

As everything on the face of the earth exists to help us to do this, we must appreciate and make use of everything that helps, and rid ourselves of anything that is destructive to our living in love in his presence.

Therefore we must be so poised (detached/indifferent) that we do not cling to any created thing as though it were our ultimate good, but remain open to the possibility that love may demand of us poverty rather than riches, sickness rather than health, dishonour rather than honour, a short life rather than a long one, because God alone is our security, refuge and strength.

We can be so detached from any created thing only if we have a stronger attachment; therefore our one dominating desire and fundamental choice must be to live in love in his presence.

6

Changing Direction

Repent, and believe the Good News.   (Mark 1:15)

When God, in Christ, says 'Repent and believe the Good News', he is uttering an invitation, not a threat. It is as though he is saying to us, 'Come and see what I want to give you and you will find that it goes beyond your wildest dreams and imaginings. You are being cruel to yourself in the way you are living at present. Come out of the prison of your tomb, break down the walls of your false securities, and come with me, so that you and I can live as one undivided person.'

Repentance is accepting this invitation, sin is the refusal to accept it. In St John's account of the Last Supper, Jesus promises his disciples that after his death the Spirit will come, 'And when he comes, he will show the world how wrong it was about sin . . . about sin: proved by their refusal to believe in me' (John 16:8–9).

Unless we repent we cannot discover the treasure. Failure to repent is the root cause of the evils which beset Christians individually and as a Church. Without repentance we become idolators of wealth, status, power, although we may still claim to be religious people. Idolators become what they worship – empty, meaningless and inhuman.

However, the truth that without repentance we lapse into idolatry has to be balanced by another, namely that we are all pilgrims and no one, this side of death, can claim to have a spirit of complete repentance, just as no one can claim to have attained complete self-knowledge. There are layers upon layers of consciousness within us and on our journey towards God we are constantly discovering areas of atheism within us, provided we dare to look. These discoveries are signs of progress, not of failure. That is why so many of the saints, guilty of no serious wrongdoing in their lives, think of them- · selves as great sinners. They have reached inner depths of sinfulness in themselves of which most of us are blissfully unaware. They are amazed and full of gratitude to God, who accepts them in their darkness and sinfulness, while those of us who have not reached those depths may be delighted and full of gratitude at our own virtuous respectability. If we are genuinely to repent, we must acknowledge our own sinfulness and powerlessness. Christ's command, 'Repent,' is a call to recognize our own sinfulness and to entrust ourselves to God's goodness and mercy: it does not mean that everyone who has not yet eradicated all their sinfulness is an idolator, a truth which Jesus illustrated clearly in the parable of the Pharisee and the tax collector who go up to the temple to pray (Luke 18:10–14).

'I thank you God [says the Pharisee], that I am not grasping, unjust, adulterous like the rest of mankind, and particularly that I am not like this tax collector here. I fast twice a week; I pay tithes on all I get.' The tax collector stood some distance away, not daring even to raise his eyes to heaven, but he beat his breast and said 'God, be merciful to me, a sinner.' 'This man [Jesus said] went home again at rights with God: the other did not.'

It is the tax collector who has repented and is in a right relationship with God: the virtuous Pharisee has not repented and is locked into his own complacency. The tax collector, no doubt, has still to struggle with his greed and lust, perhaps more than the Pharisee, but he is at rights with God because he acknowledges his own sinfulness and helplessness, puts his trust in God's power and asks for mercy. The Pharisee is not aware of his need for God, for he has found his security in his own respectability.

One reason for our failure to repent is our misunderstanding of its meaning. In an earlier chapter we looked at some false images of God, including God presented as the monstrous Uncle George. Corresponding to a false image of God, we can also have false ideas about the meaning of sin and repentance. Many Christians bemoan our present age and maintain that it has lost all sense of sin. Whenever such complaints are made it is important to discover what the speaker means by sin, for the sense of sin, whose absence is so bitterly bewailed, is often itself sinful, and its disappearance should be a cause of thanksgiving, to be bewailed only by those whose joy is in destruction. In illustrating this point I shall take examples from the Roman Catholic Church, but the same false notions of sin and repentance are to be found in other Christian Churches.

In the Roman Catholic Church bad teaching in the institutional stage of religion can leave the impression on childrens' and adults' minds that God, in his infinite mercy, has sown a thick minefield in this vale of tears, entrusted the minefield's map only to the teaching authority of the Church, understood as meaning the Pope, the bishops and the clergy, who then communicate this knowledge to those who attend Catholic schools and go to Mass on Sundays.

The minefields are of two kinds: those which damage the soul, but not fatally, and are called 'venial sins', and those which kill the soul and are called 'mortal sins'. To step on this latter type of minefield is to blow up your immortal soul. The soul is presented as being an invisible, intangible entity, knowable only by faith. Consequently, when the mine detonates, the disaster is not immediately perceived, but if we die without 'repenting' and, if possible, receiving the Sacrament of Reconciliation, we shall have an eternity in hell in which to realize the heinousness of the crime we have committed. The opportunities which life provides for stepping on one of these minefields are innumerable. For Catholics, quite apart from the major crimes which would bring a life-sentence in any respectable criminal court, there are many other acts and omissions which can incur an eternal sentence in conditions which would make the Gulag Archipelago seem like a luxury hotel in comparison. Deliberately missing Mass on Sunday or 'wilful pleasure in the irregular motions of the flesh' brought the same penalty as torture and mass murder. When I was ordained a deacon in 1958, we were told that we were now bound under mortal sin to recite daily the breviary, a series of psalms, readings and prayers. The daily breviary had seven parts. Deliberate omission of any one part was a mortal sin. We had, therefore, seven additional minefields to negotiate daily!

Alongside this teaching there developed a most complex casuistry to enable the pilgrim people of God to know how near they might approach to a minefield without actually being blown up. Deliberately missing Mass on Sundays was a mortal sin, but if you lived more than three miles walking distance from the Church, of if you were ill, or you were a farmer and would lose your crop if not harvested immediately, or you were likely to meet someone at Mass who might be a serious occasion of sin, then you could be excused from the obligation!

The damage done to a sensitive and imaginative person by this kind of teaching is tragic and a perversion of the Good News. Having listened to one particular person who had suffered inner torture through this kind of teaching, I was not at all surprised when, in answer to my question, 'If you were completely free of all moral obligations, what would you most like to do?', she answered, 'Burn down churches'.

As I write, I can hear comment in part of my mind saying, 'This is wild exaggeration and a gross distortion of Catholic moral teaching.' I agree that it is distortion, but this distortion has been communicated to many, has caused mental break-down or disillusionment, has fuelled anxiety neuroses, stunted moral development and has so filled some people with guilt that they now feel bad about feeling good, and all spontaneity, delight and joy has been banished from their lives.

Another voice says, 'You have given an out-dated tirade against a form of teaching which is no longer given today.' I hope this objection is valid and that such teaching is no longer given today, but we are still suffering from its effects. Catholic morality is still, in spite of the documents of the Second Vatican Council and the excellent social encyclicals of recent popes, too selective and individualist: selective in its emphasis on sexual morality, especially contraception and abortion, which is not matched by an equally vigorous emphasis on the evils of planning the mass extermination of millions of human beings; and individualist because awareness of our responsibility, not just for our own lives, but also for the life of the society in which we live, is still foreign to most Christians. One of the signs that we really have lost a sense of sin and a spirit of repentance is the selective nature of our moral teaching, its individualist emphasis, which ignores our corporate responsibility for the sin of the world, and its condemnatory tone.

Two years ago I spent a few months in South Africa. One Sunday afternoon I had a conversation with a black woman, who lived in Soweto, the black township on the outskirts of Johannesberg. She was elderly, her face heavily lined, her eyes sad, as though she bore in her person the sufferings of her race. She spoke slowly at first, of her bitterness at being forced to live in Soweto (a labour pool for Johannesberg of more than one and a half million blacks) and of her even greater fear of losing her job and being deported to a 'homeland', poor land which was not her home. As there was a danger of drought at the time, her water had been cut off in Soweto and now water had to be bought. That same evening I celebrated Mass in a white area of Johannesberg, where a white doctor addressed the congregation on the evils of abortion. He obviously felt very strongly and reeled off statistics, but he said not a word about the social conditions, the unemployment and lack of housing which led many, who wanted to have children, to have an abortion instead. Nor did he make any mention of the inhuman conditions in which many of the Africans and Coloureds in South Africa are forced to live while deprived of any political voice, although they form over 80 per cent of the country's population. The doctor's address was selective in its exclusive emphasis on the evils of abortion without any reference to its underlying causes, condemnatory in its failure to show any understanding of the pressures which lead people to have abortions, and self-righteous in failing to give any hint that both he and the congregation might be colluding in the crime which he so vigorously denounced.

To make sin synonymous with wrongdoing is to rob it of its meaning. If sin is considered to be the same thing as wrongdoing, then St Paul before his conversion was sinless, for he observed the Law with great exactitude, 'As far as the Law can make you perfect, I was faultless' (Phil. 3:6). To urge people to 'Obedience, diligence, honesty, order, cleanliness, temperance, truthfulness, sacrifice and love of one's country' may seem to be a call to repentance: in fact, the quotation is taken from an inscription on the ceiling of one of the administration buildings in Dachau, the Nazi concentration camp, for prisoners to read frequently. It was a call to idolatry of the Third Reich, not a call to turn to God.

To repent, or do penance, is not simply to renounce certain kinds of wrongdoing (although it will include this), or to deny ourselves certain legitimate pleasures, or to inflict pain on ourselves, or to be more strict in observing the rules of our Church. It is possible to be very wicked and destructive while at the same time being very ascetic in our personal way of life: a church-going, non-smoking teetotaller who eats sparingly may also be an unscrupulous torturer and murderer. 'Repentance' is the translation of a Greek word, 'metanoia', which means a change of mind and heart, a change of outlook. If, for example, I am emerging from a nightmare in which I have been hearing bloodcurdling roars and seeing grotesque giants lurking in the shadows and ready to leap on me, and then I awake to hear the roar of the wind and see the shadows of waving branches playing on the bedroom wall by the light of the moon, this process of awakening from dream to reality may be described as 'repentance' in the original meaning of the word, namely, a change of outlook.

To believe as a Christian is not primarily to assent to propositions of the Christian creed: primarily, to believe is to entrust our whole being to God. When people marry, their assent is not primarily to the propositions of the marriage ceremony, but to each other. To repent and believe the Good News is to turn away from self-idolatry and to let God be God in us, the God of compassion, who so loves all that he has created that he came to us in Jesus and gave his life for the life of all of us. One of the signs of true repentance in an individual, or in the Church, is the spirit of compassion for all creation which permeates their morality. Selective morality, which emphasizes, for example, the sacredness of property rights and punishes any infringement more severely than infringement of human rights, or which emphasizes sexual morality but remains blind to, or silent about, the destruction of human life through financial greed or false patriotism, can be a subtle way of protecting ourselves from God and from his demands, and is a sign of our failure to repent.

Sin, the refusal to let God be God, lies deep in our nature. We tend to think that if only our bodily appetites were controlled and in harmony, we should be without sin, but our sinfulness is deeper than our bodily appetites, a truth expressed in Christianity in the account of the fall of the angels. The greatest sin of which we are capable lies not in the body, but in our spirit, the sin of pride, a deep-seated tendency to live as though all creation should praise, reverence and serve us and our interests. Because the tendency is so deep-seated, the Church teaches that our lives must be a continual penance, that is, a constant struggle to change the direction of our lives from preoccupation with our own security to letting God be our only security. There is a good illustration of this human tendency to imprison ourselves in our own tomb of pride in Tolstoy's novel *Resurrection*, in which he describes the attitude of the prostitute Katusha:

It is usually imagined that a thief, a murderer, a spy, a prostitute, acknowledging his or her profession to be evil, is ashamed of it. But the contrary is true. People whom fate or their own sin-mistakes have placed in a certain position, however false that position may be, form a view of life in general which makes their position seem good and admissible. In order to keep their view of life, these people keep instinctively to the circle of those who share their views of life and their own place in it. This surprises us where the persons are thieves bragging about their dexterity, prostitutes vaunting their depravity, or murderers boasting of their cruelty. But it surprises us only because the circle, the atmosphere, in which these people live, is limited, and chiefly because we are outside it. Can we not observe the same phenomenon when the rich boast of their wealth – robbery; when the commanders of armies pride themselves on their victories – murder; when those in high places vaunt their power – violence? That we do not see the perversion in the views of life held by these people is only because the circle formed by them is larger and we ourselves belong to it . . .

Katusha, the prostitute, saw herself as a very important person, and Tolstoy continues:

She prized this view more than anything else; she could not but prize it, for if she lost this view of life, she would

70

lose the importance it accorded her. And in order not to lose the meaning of life, she instinctively clung to the set that looked at life in the same way as she did.

Katusha's fear is the fear of every human being, the fear of our own meaninglessness and nothingness. All of us, in our different ways, struggle to defend ourselves against this fear, building up our individual and corporate defences. This is a healthy instinct, necessary for human growth and development. The danger is that we begin to use the defences not as a means to human growth, but as a protection against it. In Christian understanding all our defences are provisional, and legitimate only in so far as they enable us to grow into an at-one-ness with God. 'The other things on the face of the earth are created for man to help him in attaining the end for which he is created. Hence, man is to make use of them in as far as they help him in the attainment of his end, and he must rid himself of them in as far as they prove a hindrance to him.' Making our defences ends in themselves is to turn them into defences against God. Our defences have become our idols, our false gods, and this is the root of all sin. That is why the first commandment is 'Thou shalt not have false gods before me', and all the other commandments follow from this.

We misread our fear of meaninglessness. It is not a threat of annihilation, but an invitation to face truth. The facts are kind, and God is in the facts. The fear of our own meaninglessness is saying to us: 'Your defences are ultimately useless. You are wrong in judging your worth by the strength of your useless defences. God alone is your rock, your refuge and your strength. Acknowledge that truth and you will come to know your real worth, for you are precious in his eyes and he loves you. He is calling you to share his own life.' Sin is our refusal to accept this invitation; we prefer our own security. We are like Lazarus in our tombs. God calls us out to life. We reply, 'Thank you, but I prefer to stay where I am.'

From within the ring of our own defences against God, we can look with disapproval at those within other security rings which may threaten us. We do this as individuals, as groups and as nations. If we are religiously inclined, we may bring God within our defence ring, declaring atheist and evil any who may threaten our security. In God's name we threaten to annihilate any who endanger our defences, and God becomes the justification of our thefts, our violence and our murder, which we now call preservation of our freedom and sovereignty, the upkeep of law and order, and patriotism. We become selective in our morality, foster an individualist morality which does not look beyond the perimeter of its own defence lines, and we become increasingly convinced of our own self-righteousness.

The Old Testament prophets were constantly attacking the false securities of Israel, especially Israel's attempts to justify its behaviour by using God, feeling safe because it practised religious ritual and external observances. God, through the prophet Isaiah, says to them:

> What are your endless sacrifices to me? I am sick of holo-causts of rams and the fat of calves. The blood of bulls and goats revolts me. . . . Bring me your worthless offerings no more, the smoke of them fills me with disgust. New moons, sabbaths, assemblies – I cannot endure festival and solem-nity. Your new moons and pilgrimages I hate with all my soul. They lie heavy on me. I am tired of bearing them. When you stretch out your hands I turn my eyes away. You may multiply your prayers, I will not listen. Your hands are covered with blood, wash, make yourselves clean. Take your wrong-doing out of my sight. Cease to do evil. Learn to do good, search for justice, help the oppressed, be just to the orphan, plead for the widow. (Isa. 1:11–17)

Christ, the fulfilment of the prophets, continues their message, warning against the evil of finding security in wealth. 'It is easier for a camel to pass through the eye of a needle than for a rich man to enter the kingdom of heaven.' Even more dangerous than security in wealth is the security of our own self-righteousness when we reject God while at the same time claiming him in defence of our rejection. Gentle Jesus is vitriolic in his condemnation of this false security, calling those who practise it hypocrites, whited sepulchres, people who shut the kingdom of God in other peoples' faces, neither going in themselves nor allowing others to go in, people who strain at gnats and swallow camels. Jesus, image of the God we cannot see, is gentle with those who sin through weakness and who acknowledge their evil. He is harsh with those who consider themselves righteous, because they are abusing God, making him the justification of their evil deeds. Jesus welcomed sinners and dined with them. It was religious men who, with the co-operation of those responsible for law and order, crucified him as a blasphemer.

Jesus sums up his own teaching in the first of the beatitudes: 'Blessed [that is, 'blissfully happy'] are you who are poor: yours is the kingdom of heaven.' Blissfully happy are you who know your own emptiness and throw yourselves on the mercy of God. The opposite state is described in Luke's Gospel: 'But alas for you who are rich: you are having your consolation now.' 'Rich' refers not only to material possessions, but to that attitude of mind and heart which finds its ultimate security in anything that is not God. That is why religious people, closed in their own religiosity, are greater sinners than 'the tax gatherers and prostitutes'. Sin is destructive of human life. It is worth noting that the most violent conflicts today are among people with strong religious beliefs, convinced that God is on their side as they murder their enemies – in Northern Ireland, Lebanon, Iran and Iraq, South Africa.

Sin is the refusal to let God be God.
Repentance is letting God be God in our lives.

Knowing our sinfulness and repenting is a lifelong, continual process. We can never reach a stage before death when we no longer need repentance, because there are layers upon layers of consciousness within us, and each moment of existence can reveal these layers, if we let it, and show us the depth of the tendency within us to refuse to let God be God.

God is gentle. He gradually reveals our sinfulness to us. He does not seem to worry about our past wrongdoing, even though its effects may still be causing suffering to ourselves and others. 'Though your sins are like scarlet, they shall be as white as snow' (Isa. 1:18). What does concern him is the direction in which we are moving. If we turn towards him, no matter how far away we may be, he reaches out to welcome us. Our real sin is in refusing, or fearing to turn back, either because we are quite content with ourselves as we are, or because we think we must first put ourselves in order before we can turn to him.

What may appear to us as a reason for despair – some

failure, loss of job, reputation, disgrace, persistent moral weakness, physical or mental illness, failure in a marriage or religious vocation – can become a moment of grace and the beginning of a new life, if only we can acknowledge our failure and turn trustingly to God. The answer is in the pain and no human state is ever hopeless.

This chapter can best be summarized by comparing some characteristics of true repentance with signs of false repentance. If, in reading what follows, you think your own disposition is more accurately described under the heading of false repentance, do not despair, but use the discovery as the tax collector used his knowledge of his own sinfulness, namely as a springboard towards God. Remember, too, that repentance is a gradual process, a lifelong work, and that in all of us there will always be a mixture of true and false repentance. What is important is that we should acknowledge our need of God.

Marks of true repentance	*Marks of false repentance*
True repentance frees from self-preoccupation because our trust is in God's goodness working in us. In his light we see our darkness.	False repentance immerses us in self-preoccupation. We delight in what we consider our virtue but are irritated by our vice, refuse to acknowledge it and project it on to others.
True repentance brings joy and inner freedom.	False repentance increases anxiety and makes us more defensive.
True repentance can welcome criticism and learn from it.	False repentance is touchy about criticism and learns nothing from it.
True repentance brings understanding, tolerance and hope.	False repentance engenders a rigidity of mind and heart, dogmatism, intolerance and a condemnatory attitude.
True repentance brings compassion and therefore a	False repentance is sensitive to justice only in so far as it

sharpened sensitivity to all forms of injustice.

promotes the interest of the individual or his group and is therefore selective in its moral condemnation.

True repentance shares God's laughter and frees the mind to see the humour of all situations.

False repentance tends to be over serious and cannot laugh at itself.

In true repentance a person feels drawn to God.

In false repentance a person feels driven by God.

These characteristic qualities apply not only to individuals within a Church, but also to the Church itself:

A Church with a spirit of true repentance will be concerned primarily with its mission, not its maintenance. It will see all its securities as provisional, finding its one security in God.

A Church with a spirit of false repentance will be primarily concerned with its own maintenance, whether of its doctrinal or moral orthodoxy, or of its prestige in society, the preservation of its own structures or of its material possessions.

A Church with a true spirit of repentance will encourage the critical and mystical elements as well as the institutional in its members.

A Church which has no true spirit of repentance will emphasize the institutional element and give little or no encouragement to the critical and mystical.

The Church is to be 'a Light to the Nations'. What is true of the Church and of individuals within it, will also be true of any group, institution, nation, whether religious or secular.

A nation with a spirit of true repentance, besides the above characteristics, will pay particular attention to the quality of life of all its members which is compat-

A nation without a spirit of repentance will be chiefly concerned with its own wealth and international status. The health of its economy and the strength of

ible with the quality of life of other nations. If a spirit of penitence takes hold of a nation it will abhor any form of narrow nationalism, just as an individual who is really penitent abhors egoism.

its defence system will be its main preoccupation. If the nation has a religious tradition, religion will be used to confirm its security policies.

There are no exercises at the end of this chapter. Reading and writing about sin and penance does not necessarily give us any felt knowledge of our own and the world's sinfulness. God alone can teach us what sin is and he alone can draw us to himself in penance. The following chapter is a chapter of exercises, ways of coming to know God's goodness at work in the darkness of our own lives and in the life of the world, and of experiencing something of the inner joy and freedom which true repentance brings.

7

Beginning to Dig for the Treasure

Since, tho' he is under the world's splendour and wonder,
　　His mystery must be instressed, stressed;
For I greet him the days I meet him, and bless when I understand.
　　　　　　　(G. M. Hopkins, 'The Wreck of the Deutschland')

Sin is the refusal to let God be God. One subtle way of refusing, while pretending not to, is so to emphasize the 'otherness' of God that for all practical purposes he ceases to matter. In Greek mythology, Cerberus was a three-headed guard dog of the underworld, whose murderous attentions could be diverted by offering him honeyed cakes. We do the same with God, offering him the honeyed cakes of our Sunday rituals, uttering honeyed words of our heartfelt devotion, trusting that this action will keep God at bay for the coming week. This is a refusal to let God be the God of all things, who is continuously drawing us to himself in every breath we breathe. Baptism is our celebration of this truth, a universal truth, for God calls every human being to himself.

If it is true that God is at work in every detail of our lives, how do we begin to recognize his action and our reaction, for 'tho' he is under the world's splendour and wonder, his mystery must be instressed, stressed'? One way is to practise daily the following exercise, called 'A Review of Consciousness'.

At the end of a day, especially before going to sleep, the mind, without any conscious effort on our part, tends to play back some of the events of the day so vividly that if the day has been particularly eventful we can find it difficult to get to sleep. We may find ourselves re-enacting a quarrel, thinking of the clever and cutting things we might have said if only we had been more quick-witted. The review of consciousness is based on this natural tendency of the mind.

Before beginning any prayer, it is good to spend a few seconds reminding ourselves what we are about to do, then asking God that our whole being may be directed purely to his service and praise. It is a prayer that our life 'may be directed', and so we can make it although we may be very aware that, in fact, it is not so directed.

Having made this prayer, then let your mind drift over the day, refraining from any self-judgement, whether of approval or disapproval, attending to and relishing only those moments of the day for which you are grateful. Even the most harrowing day includes some good moments, if only we take the trouble to look – it might be the sight of a raindrop falling, or the fact than I can see at all. When people attempt this exercise, they are usually surprised at the number and variety of good moments in the day which, had they not deliberately recalled them, would have been quickly forgotten, obscured, perhaps, by any painful experience in the day. This daily review of consciousness is an exercise in 'the praise, reverence and service of God'. Having remembered the events for which you are grateful, thank and praise God for them.

After thanksgiving, the next step is to recall your inner moods and feelings, noting, if you can, what occasioned them, but again refraining from any self-judgement. Be with Christ as you look at these moods and beg him to show you the attitudes which underlie them. For your part, do not try to analyse the moods: just relive, in Christ's presence, the events which gave rise to them. Contemplate the events of the day and pray to Christ out of your experience of them. Sometimes, this can be very painful, for if we look at the scene and refrain from judging, the facts can begin to judge us and we can begin to see with clarity our own refusal to understand, listen, be compassionate and treat the other person, or persons, with love. Because they would not take their place in our kingdom of values, praising, reverencing and serving us and our ideas, we rejected them. The important thing is not to analyse our experience, but to contemplate it in Christ's presence and let him show us where we have let him be in us and where we have refused to let him be. Thank him for the times we have 'let his glory through' and beg his forgiveness for the times we have refused him entry. He never refuses forgiveness. He knows our weakness far better than we do. All that we have to do is show it to him and he can transform our weakness into strength.

Finally, look briefly at the day ahead and beg him to be with us in every detail of it. The whole exercise should not take more than fifteen minutes, but it is a most valuable fifteen minutes and, if practised daily, we become more sensitive to his action in our lives not only at the time of the exercise, but also in the middle of our activities. Do not expect miracles in the first week, or even in the first month, but the effects will become apparent. We shall find that he is making us more able to love, to experience a joy welling up within us, often unexpectedly. We shall become less agitated and more peaceful, less hurried and more content to wait, less suspicious and more ready to trust, able to find interest and delight in people who used to make us bristle, less fearful of what others may think of us and more free to be ourselves, kinder to others and to ourselves and less likely to fly off the handle.

The next exercise is an imaginative contemplation and I shall give one example in detail, using Christ's parable of the Two Sons, the prodigal and his elder brother, in order to illustrate the method. Further Scripture passages suitable for prayer on finding God in our darkness and knowing the joy of his forgiveness are given at the end of the chapter. This type of exercise requires 30–60 minutes. Before beginning, decide how long you are going to spend on it. If you have decided on 40 minutes and after ten of them you think you are getting nowhere and want to abandon the prayer, do not give up but stay with it for the forty minutes. This is not an exercise in self-control: it is far more important than that. There are layers upon layers of consciousness within us. Very frequently the preliminary state before reaching a deeper layer is a feeling of inner emptiness, dryness and boredom. If we abandon the prayer every time we feel bored, we never reach the deeper layers. Few people can find the time to do these exercises daily. They can be valuable, however infrequently you may do them.

Before beginning the prayer, read over chapter 15 of St Luke's Gospel, re-reading the parable of the Two Sons until you are familiar with the content.

Begin the prayer, as in the first exercise, by asking God that all that is within you may be directed purely to his service and praise during this period of prayer and ask, too, for a deepening knowledge and sorrow for sin.

Now let your imagination play on the passage and pray out of whatever you experience. That is the essence of the method and what follows is only an elaboration of that statement.

'The tax collectors and the sinners, meanwhile, were all seeking his company to hear what he had to say, and the Pharisees and the scribes complained. "This man", they said, "welcomes sinners and eats with them." ' Be there with this group of men and women. Have a good look at them, their features, gestures, their eyes, how they are dressed. Talk with some of them, ask what all the excitement is about and why they are so attracted by Christ. Look at Christ, too, how he receives them, how he greets them and how he greets you. Watch the scribes and Pharisees approach and listen to what they are saying about Christ and how he reacts to them. You may find this part of the scene holds your attention. If so, stay with it as long as you can before moving on, for the object of the prayer is not to cover a syllabus, but to encounter God within you through the medium of the Scripture passage.

You may find you cannot get started and your mind keeps jumping from one thought to another. You may be afflicted with doubts of faith (Do I really believe in God, in the Scripture?) or doubt about your own sincerity (Do I really want to have sorrow for sin?) or you may feel overwhelmed with guilt and feelings of hopelessness. Treat all these thoughts and feelings as you treated them in the awareness exercises, acknowledging that they are present but bringing yourself gently back to the scene and refusing to tangle with them. If you are unable to focus your attention on the scene, pretend you are describing it to someone else and you may find yourself quickly engaged in it. If this does not help and your mind continues to jump about, then show Christ your scattered mind and distracted heart and ask that his Spirit should hover over your inner chaos as the Spirit hovered over the chaos at the beginning of creation, bringing life and order out of it. The Spirit is always hovering over our chaos. When we pray, we may become more aware of our inner chaos.

This is a grace, a gift of insight, not a sign of failure. Acknow-ledging the chaos and submitting it to Christ can lead us to deep repentance, deeper perhaps than would have been poss-ible if we had floated through the prayer on a flood of more superficial feeling.

As you watch the Pharisees and scribes complain about Christ's conduct and watch his reaction, you might ask your-self whether these same complaints are being made today. You may find that your sympathies are with the Pharisees and so discover attitudes in yourself of which you were previously unaware.

Listen to Christ as he describes with three parables, the parable of the Lost Sheep, of the Lost Drachma and of the Two Lost Sons, God's attitude to sinners, the God who at this moment holds me in being, who feels more for me than I can possibly feel for him, or for anyone, the God who leaves the ninety-nine sheep and searches for the lost one, who scours creation to find me as the woman scours her house to find the lost drachma. The mystic, St Catherine of Genoa, once said, 'God seems to have nothing else to do than to unite himself to us,' and an even more surprising statement, 'It seems to me that God has no other business than myself'!

As Christ tells the story of the two sons, use your imagin-ation on the story so that you see the younger son leaving his father's house with his inheritance. Talk with him as he travels abroad of his hopes and expectations, see his initial delight until the money runs out, his friends disappear and he is sitting in the pig-sty. He is a symbol of all of us who have used our inheritance, our minds and bodies, to ensure that as much of creation as possible should praise, reverence and serve us. Contemplating him in the pig-sty can put us in touch with our own inner emptiness.

The prodigal decides to return home not from any high and honourable motive, but simply because he is hungry and desperate. This is a most consoling truth. His father is watching for him and rushes to meet him, not because the son is virtuous, nor because his motives are pure, but simply because he is his son and has returned home. All that we have to do is to admit our own emptiness to God and he rushes out to meet us. Linger on this truth because it is letting God be God to us, whereas our tendency is to want to put ourselves in order before we meet him, to be more conscious of our guilt than of his goodness. As you watch the encounter between father and son, beg to know that this truth is happening in you now, that you are embraced and kissed by the father who delights in you. Let this truth break in on your unbelief and speak to the father from your heart with the simplicity of a child.

When you are ready to move on, go out and meet the elder son coming home from work in the fields and talk with him. Watch his reaction to the sounds of music and dancing coming from the house and hear what he has to say when the servant tells him the reason for the celebration. He is so angry and bitter that when his father comes out to persuade him to enter and join the feast, he disowns both his father and brother saying, 'You, and that son of yours'. Try to feel the indignation and bitterness of the elder brother, for we may discover that it resonates with hidden anger and bitterness in our own hearts. The elder brother is so conscious of his own hard work and dutiful service that he despises anyone who does not match up to him, and he resents any leniency being shown to weaker and less conscientious people. His treasure is in his own goodness, as exemplified in his own life, and so he cannot recognize any other goodness. He typifies the Pharisees' attitude, which Christ describes as blindness. Ponder this attitude, see it still operative in the twentieth century and perhaps see it, with horror, as describing ourselves. The father does not tirade against this arrogance and blindness: he simply says, 'My son, you are with me always, and all I have is yours,' words which are being spoken to me now.

I have written at length on this parable, not to suggest that this is the way you should contemplate the passage, but simply to illustrate something of the wealth there is in any passage of the Gospel if it is pondered imaginatively. In praying such a passage, the longer you can linger on one image or phrase the better, and the prayer should never be hurried.

When you have finished the imaginative contemplation, it is useful to let it play back to you for 10–15 minutes, noticing especially the feelings which came to you unexpectedly, whether of joy, peace, hope, strength, or of boredom, doubt, anxiety, sadness. Do not attempt to analyse these feelings, but note, if you can, what it was in the contemplation which gave rise to them. Note, too, any part of the prayer in which you felt your mind go blank, or where you seemed to be blocked.

The next time you pray, instead of moving on to another Scripture text, return to this passage and begin with those images, phrases, or words which you found helpful, remaining with them as long as you can. Then look at the parts of the prayer when you experienced negative feelings of anxiety, sadness, etc., and show them to Christ. These negative feelings are not signs of failure, but of discovery, and they can be as valuable as, sometimes more valuable than, the more positive feelings. It may be, for example, that some can contemplate the first part of the parable, delight in the meeting between the father and the son, but experience anxiety or go blank as soon as they attempt to look at the elder son. This might signify a deep, subconscious reluctance to face the truth of their own pharisaism. Until they do so, they cannot be freed from it, nor know the joy of hearing God say, 'All I have is yours'.

How long should you spend in praying passages of Scripture suited to deepening your knowledge of and sorrow for sin? The answer to that question is within you, so move on when you feel ready to move on. Gratitude to God for his forgiveness will lead you to ask him to know him more and to serve him with all your being. Our progress towards God is cyclic, like climbing a spiral staircase. You may find yourself later wanting to return to spending time on prayer for sorrow and repentance because you have reached a deeper level of awareness of God's goodness which reveals areas of unbelief in your life which you had never noticed before.

There are two obstacles frequently encountered at the start of our journey towards God which can be very difficult to surmount, namely feelings of guilt and self-worthlessness and also the memory of hurts done to us by others.

Guilt is a healthy human reaction to our own wrongdoing, but it can also become an unhealthy disease which poisons our spirit. When afflicted with guilt over something we have done, or failed to do, we should acknowledge our wrongdoing to Christ and beg to know his forgiveness. It is hard for us to accept unconditional love, for our human experience conditions us otherwise, leading us to think that love must be earned and that we can be acceptable to others only in so far as we measure up to their expectations of us. God's love is unconditional: all that we have to do is to turn to him. We may be like the Gerasene demoniac, torn in our repentance, part of us wanting it, part not. Pray out of that part of you which wants to repent and do not let the other part deter you. 'Catching sight of Jesus from a distance, he ran up and fell at his feet and shouted at the top of his voice, "What do you want with me, Jesus, son of the Most High God? Swear by God you will not torture me" ' (Mark 5:6–7).

Persistent and pervasive guilt, which cannot be located in any particular action or omission, is a sickness of the spirit and is usually accompanied by feelings of worthlessness, of being unloved and unlovable. Victims of this illness feel they must be constantly apologizing for their existence, feel they must always try to please, yet know that no matter how hard they try, they will never be acceptable to any human being, least of all to God. The root of this illness may lie in childhood deprivation by parents who showed little or no affection, but were constantly punishing the child, assuring it of its worthlessness and wickedness. The child may so assimilate the attitude of its parents that this attitude becomes a permanent assumption of its mind, a super-ego, so that even in adulthood the person lives in a permanent state of guilt and anxiety. This is a severe affliction, but the following method of prayer can reveal a deeper meaning and a way of understanding and growing through the affliction.

Salvador Dali has painted the crucified Christ suspended above the globe of the earth. Let your imagination work on that image and speak to Christ dying on the cross. He has become the sin of the world and there is no crime, however hideous, which he has not taken on himself and forgiven. Tell Christ that although he has succeeded with the rest of the human race, he has met his match in you, and that not even his death can overcome your guilt. He may find all other human beings to be lovable, but you are God's mistake which he can never put right. If you can persist in this prayer, he will uncover a hidden source of guilt, which is pride, the refusal to let God be God to you, clinging to your guilt as though it were more powerful than his love.

Another method is to sit in silence with your feelings of guilt and worthlessness, as though they formed a heap of rotting rubbish in front of you and then pray to Christ to show himself through the mess. This is a useful exercise because in it you are not pretending, not hiding your guilt from yourself; you are acknowledging your own inability to remove it and allowing him to be what we can so easily express with our lips, but not with our inner being – our saviour.

The memory of hurts done to us in the past can also become obstacles in our journey towards God. 'Anyone who says, "I love God", and hates his brother, is a liar' (1 John 4:20). It is very difficult to forgive from the heart, but as long as we withhold forgiveness we are refusing to let God be God in us.

Everything that we experience registers in our being and affects all our subsequent perception of reality, and it therefore affects the way we think, act and react, although we may be completely unaware of the reasons for our behaviour. The events which fashioned our way of perceiving are buried deep in our subconscious memory. That is why, for example, certain sounds, smells, sights can greatly affect us while the people we are with seem unaffected by them. The reason may be that those sense impressions have touched hidden memories in us, perhaps from childhood, when we experienced great happiness and the smell, sight, or sound has touched off the feeling of happiness, although our memory can no longer recall the incident itself. Similarly, present events may throw us into gloom, sadness or anxiety while they leave other people relatively unmoved. We cannot understand our reaction, because we cannot recall the painful incident in the past. The mind recalls the pain, but not the past event which caused it. In imaginative contemplation hidden memories often surface, including the memory of past hurts, and we may see for the first time, how the whole of our subsequent life has been affected by those events. The person troubled by permanent guilt feelings, for example, may suddenly come to realize that parents were to blame. It can then be very difficult to forgive them for having blighted his/ her life. The temptation is to ignore this knowledge and the feelings accompanying it because they are too painful to face. The temptation should be resisted.

We need to pray over these memories in order to be released from the stifling effect they are having on our lives, whether they have suddenly come into consciousness or have always been there. Imaginative contemplation on the Gospel's healing miracles are useful for this purpose. Be there in imagination at the healing, then approach Christ and ask healing for your own hurt, ailment, or handicap. Through the medium of the Gospel passage you are encountering the Living Christ now.

Past hurts can go very deep, so do not be surprised if, having prayed for healing from the heart, having managed to forgive those concerned and experienced peace and freedom, the pain of the hurt should return again later. It takes time for the bitterness and hurt to be drawn from the deeper levels of our mind and heart.

If contemplating a Gospel passage does not help you to face the bitterness and hurt, then imagine you are in a room by yourself and there is a knock at the door. 'Look, I am standing at the door, knocking. If one of you hears me calling and opens the door, I will come in to share his meal, side by side with him' (Rev. 3:20). In imagination, take Christ on a tour of the house, which is your life. Take him into those rooms, that is, those events, in which you experienced great pain and introduce him to the people who caused it. Express to them, even although they may now be dead, and to Christ, the hurt you still feel and then look at him and see how he reacts to the people concerned. Do not force yourself into insincere gestures or words of forgiveness, but rather let him draw the feelings and the words out of you. Even if you can only say, 'I want to want to be able to forgive,' that is progress. In the same way, you can ask forgiveness of those you have offended.

The effect such prayer can have is astonishing, lifting heavy burdens from peoples' lives, bringing back to them a capacity for joy and delight in life which may have been stifled for years and, in some cases, restoring to physical health people who had been suffering for years from illnesses which did not respond to medical treatment.

Before proceeding any further, it may be useful to pause for a few paragraphs and review our route so far:

Jesus said, 'The kingdom of heaven is like treasure hidden in a field' – the field is you.

Inigo of Loyola caught a glimpse of the treasure within him by noticing the after-effects of his daydreams. The treasure lies in our inner life of thoughts, feelings, memories. It is our inner life which determines the way we perceive the world and react to it, both individually and corporately.

In considering the three essential elements in religion, we saw the need for each element and the harm done by ignoring any one of them. Religion can be presented with such an undue emphasis on the institutional element that it prevents us from attending to our inner life. When this happens, then it is true that 'nothing so masks the face of God as religion'.

Using Mark's account of the healing of the Gerasene demoniac, we saw something of the complexity, chaos and conflict of desires in all of us. It is over simplistic to say, 'Turn to God in prayer,' to solve the conflict, because our inner chaos affects the way we understand God, so that prayer itself can intensify our confusion. We saw that the key to our inner confusion lies in our desires.

I suggested some simple methods of prayer which can begin to reveal false images of God which may be operative in us. But the question still remained, 'How are we to avoid creating a God in our own image and likeness?'

We began to answer this question by looking at St Ignatius's 'First Principle and Foundation', whose opening sentence, 'We are created to praise, reverence and serve God,' gives the basic direction our lives must take, and the rest of his Preface outlines the disposition (indifference/detachment) necessary if we are to take it. We saw, too, that indifference/ detachment is only possible provided we have an attachment to God. He is always drawing us to himself, and that is why Christ's first message is 'Repent and believe the Good News'. 'Repent' means 'Turn to me and know my love for you'.

In this chapter we have looked at some methods of knowing God's goodness in our sinfulness. The chapter ends with a list of Scripture texts which the reader may find helpful.

I hope I have not given the impression that if you follow what has been said so far and practise a few imaginative contemplations, all your troubles will be over and you will begin a new life of bliss on earth! In the journey towards God we begin to understand the grumbling Israelites in the desert who looked back with longing to the jolly days of fleshpots in Egypt. As we turn to God, we become aware of the attractive idols in our lives which we had not noticed before, because they were part of our being. We begin to long for the carefree days when we were blind and God was a shadowy figure on the wings of our stage, ready to come in when we chose to give the cue. Now he has taken over the stage and we feel excluded from many things which used to make life worthwhile. When these feelings of regret, resentment and dislike of God's nearness afflict us, we may grow despondent and think that the effort to find him is a waste of time, or that we suffer from some inner flaw which will prevent us from ever finding him. Once we turn to God in prayer, we begin to experience fluctuations of mood and inner feeling which we may never have had before. This is a healthy sign, a sign that we are encountering the living God, the God of surprises. There is no genuine human relationship without conflict, and it is as human beings that we relate to God.

In the next chapter we shall look more closely at these varying moods, their general nature, how to react and how not to react to them.

Exercise

Some biblical texts for imaginative contemplation:

General

Genesis 3   The Adam and Eve story, when imaginatively contemplated, will be found to be very contemporary, describing the nature and effect of all sin – it separates us from ourselves, from others, from God.

Luke 15   Parable of the lost sheep, the lost drachma and the prodigal son.

John 8:34–41   Sin enslaves and blinds to truth.

Romans 7:14–25   Paul acknowledges his own helplessness.

2 Peter 2:1–22   The history and nature of sin.

James 1:13–18   The roots of sinfulness in our desires.

James 3:2—4:17   The roots of violence and disharmony.

2 Samuel 11:1—12:15   David is brought to consciousness of his own sin.

Revelation 3:14–22   On the blind complacency of the church in Laodicea.

Matthew 23:13–36   Christ's indictment of the Pharisees, included in the Gospel because the early Church was aware of its own danger of falling into Pharisaism.

Luke 18:9–14   The Pharisee and the tax collector at prayer.

Ezekiel 16   An allegorical history of Israel's infidelity and God's fidelity.

Psalms (penitential) 6; 32; 38; 51; 102; 130; 143.

In particular on social sin
Matthew 25:31–46   Jesus describes the Last Judgement.

Isaiah 1:11–19   On the uselessness of religious observance which does not spring from a heart that is compassionate and just to the poor.

Amos 5 and 6   A vitriolic attack on the affluent who live by exploiting the weak.

Luke 16:19–31   The rich man and the beggar, Lazarus.

Luke 12:16–21   The parable of the rich man who stores up treasure for himself.

Texts with particular emphasis on God's mercy and forgiveness
Luke 7:36–50   The sinner who washes Jesus' feet in the house of Simon, the Pharisee.

John 8:3–11   The adulterous woman about to be stoned.

John 13:36—14:1   Christ, immediately after foretelling Peter's denial, says: 'Do not let your hearts be troubled. Trust in God still, and trust in me.'

Isaiah 54:4–10   'Come back ... for the mountains may depart, and the hills be shaken, but my love for you will never leave you.'

Isaiah 55:1–9   God is rich in forgiving.

Some healing miracles
Mark 1:40–5   Curing a leper.

Mark 2:1–12   Curing the paralytic whose friends lower him through the roof of the house where Jesus is staying.

Mark 3:1–6   Curing a man with a withered hand.

Mark 5:1–20   The Gerasene demoniac.

Mark 5:21–41   Curing the woman with a haemorrhage and the raising of Jairus's daughter.

Mark 8:22–6   Curing a blind man.

Mark 9:14–29   Curing an epileptic boy.

John 5:1–18   Curing the man at the pool.

John 9   Curing a blind man on the sabbath.

John 11:1–44   Raising of Lazarus.

8

Recognizing the Treasure when You Find It

My God, my God, why have you forsaken me?   (Psalm 22:1)

Some hospitals now study a patient's handwriting for diag-
nostic purposes, and it is claimed that careful examination of
handwriting can reveal the beginnings of serious illness years
before it consciously affects the patient and before it is detect-
able by other methods such as X-ray. The body is transmit-
ting messages through almost imperceptible movements of
the hand. We tend to think that our intelligence is only in
our conscious minds, but our whole body is an intelligence
network and our consciousness can only grasp a small fraction, our reasoning a still smaller fraction, of what is
happening within us. Our body, feelings and emotions
respond to events more quickly and sensitively than our
reasoning minds, sometimes warning us of danger when our
conscious minds cannot detect the cause, sometimes
attracting our attention to something, or reminding us of
some past event which, at first, seems unimportant to us.

When Inigo of Loyola first began to daydream about
outdoing Francis, Dominic and Humphrey of the desert, he
had no idea of the importance for himself and for others of
what was happening to him. When he spotted the qualitative
difference in the after-effects of his daydreams – noting the
boredom, sadness and emptiness which followed his dreams
of future feats of valour and of winning the love of a great
lady, contrasting these feelings with the joy, peace and
strength which followed his dreams of outdoing the saints –
he had started on a process which he was later to call
'Discernment of Spirits', and which we might term 'Sifting our
moods and feelings' or 'Learning to read the body's signals'.

91

In his book, *Spiritual Exercises*, Ignatius gives two sets of 'Rules for the Discernment of Spirits', the first being more suited to those who are beginning the Exercises and engaged on praying for a knowledge of sin and spirit of repentance, the second set of rules being more suited to those who are contemplating the life of Christ. Ignatius knows the complexity and individuality of each human mind and so he does not claim to give rules which are absolute and covering every individual case, but he presents guidelines which can help us, to some extent at least, to begin to read our own moods and guide us in our own reaction to them. This chapter gives a shortened and simplified version of the first set of 'Rules for the Discernment of Spirits'.

In our journey towards God, our whole being reacts to the direction in which we are moving. God is continuously drawing us to himself in everything we experience.

> Yahweh, you examine me and know me,
> you know if I am standing or sitting,
> you read my thoughts from far away,
> whether I walk or lie down, you are watching,
> you know every detail of my conduct. . . .
> It was you who created my inmost self,
> and put me together in my mother's womb. (Psalm 139)

St Augustine recognized this action of God in every movement of his heart and so wrote in his Confessions, 'Thou hast created us for thyself, and our heart cannot be quieted till it may find repose in thee' (*Confessions* c. 1).

God is the answer to our inner restlessness and emptiness. When we move towards him, that is, when the fundamental option of our lives is directed to his praise, reverence and service, then our feelings and emotions resonate with this movement and we experience peace, tranquillity and joy in some measure. Whatever we do, whatever decision we make, if it is in accord with this fundamental option, then the action or decision will deepen, or at least not disturb, our peace, tranquillity and joy. If we act or decide in a way contrary to this fundamental direction, the dissonance will register somehow in our feelings, leaving us bored or anxious, agitated or sad.

In chapter 5 I compared the soul to a flock of sheep together with the sheep dog, the sheep dog representing the deepest part, the core of the soul, the sheep representing the various desires, appetites and passions within us. The good sheep dog represents the person whose fundamental option in life is the praise, reverence and service of God, but the person may have many inner desires and moods and feelings which are not integrated into this fundamental option and which will act like straying sheep. When the person tries to act, or makes a decision in accord with the fundamental option, he/she will have to snap at the heels of those elements within, which oppose this movement. The conglomerate feelings of sheep plus dog will be of agitation, weariness, sadness, boredom. When the whole operation is over and the sheep are safely through the gate, the conglomerate mood will change, and although there may be some residual soreness, there will be a general mood of peace.

If, on the other hand, the sheep dog no longer obeys its master, corresponding to a fundamental option away from God, then sheep dog and sheep may speed happily for a while towards the edge of a cliff, and only those sheep will be snapped at which attempt to move in the opposite direction. In other words, if in the core of our being we have turned away from God, then we can live quite contentedly in our selfishness for a while, our contentment disturbed only occasionally by sudden stings of conscience or remorse.

Briefly expressed, the first general guideline about interpreting our moods and inner feelings is this:

1. *If the core of our being is directed to God, then our creative moods, feelings, actions and decisions will bring peace, joy and tranquillity, while the destructive elements within us and outside us will bring agitation, sadness, inner turmoil.*

If the core of our being is turned away from God, our destructive moods, feelings, actions, and decisions will comfort and console us, while the creative elements within us and outside us will trouble and upset us with stings of conscience and remorse.

While this is a very useful general guideline, it can cause anxiety to some people, who begin to wonder whether the core of their being is God-centred or not and this doubt can cause them great inner agony. If you find yourself worrying in this way, it is a sign that the core of your soul is God-centred: if it were not, you would have no such worry.

It is also important to notice that a person who has no explicit religious belief may be, in fact, very God-centred, while another who claims religious belief and practises religious observance may be turned away from God. In St Matthew's Gospel (chapter 25), Christ describes the Final Judgement, showing that our relationship to God is expressed in our relationship to other people. 'For I was hungry and you gave me food; I was thirsty and you gave me drink; I was a stranger and you took me in, naked and you clothed me . . .' If a person is led by love of truth, justice and compassion for other people, they have found God even although they may not know his name.

This first guideline illustrates the importance of the Review of Consciousness mentioned on page 77, observing, at the end of the day, the inner moods and feelings we have experienced and asking God to enlighten us on the attitudes which underly the moods.

This first guideline can be misunderstood to mean that 'good' feelings are of God and 'bad' feelings are from evil, feelings of peace and joy etc., interpreted as from God, feelings of sadness, pain being from evil, as though those who are moving towards God must be on a perpetual high and those who are moving away from God must be chronically in low spirits. 'Bad' and negative feelings can be of God. Christ is described in St Matthew's account of the Passion, 'Sadness came over him and great distress' and he describes himself, 'My soul is sorrowful to the point of death' (Matt. 26:37). Christ weeps over Jerusalem, weeps at the death of Lazarus, becomes irritated with his disciples, 'Have you ears that cannot hear, eyes that cannot see, do you remember nothing?' Christ was not full of 'nice' feelings when he labelled the scribes and Pharisees 'hypocrites, blind guides, whited sepulchres and a brood of vipers'. He was seized with anger when he took a whip and drove the money dealers from the Temple.

Christ's negative moods of sadness, anger and irritation are the obverse of his love for the Father and for all human beings. It is because his love is so strong that his anger can be so fierce when his Father's name is desecrated and when human beings are exploited in the name of religion. These negative moods are not destructive, are not a lessening of faith, hope and charity; on the contrary, it is precisely because he is so full of faith, hope and charity that he reacts so strongly to signs of disbelief and coldness in others.

This is an important point, because in some sections of Western society, perhaps especially in religious circles, any show of feeling, especially anger, irritability, impatience, grief or sadness, is considered 'not nice', as though the ideal person should float through life with a half-Zen smile, if attracted by Eastern religions, or with a stiff upper lip, if of the Public School persuasion, untouched and untouchable by any human emotion. Anger, irritability, impatience, sadness are never wrong in themselves, but are healthy human reactions. To refuse them expression does violence to our inner selves, a violence which may be projected into aggressive behaviour towards others, or turned in on ourselves, leading to depression. The rightness or wrongness does not lie in the emotion itself, but in the underlying attitude which gives rise to the emotion. Jesus' anger, for example, with the Temple dealers was the human expression of his love for his Father's house and therefore his fury that the house of his Father should be used for exploiting the poor whom he loved and cherished. Our anger with the Temple dealers might have sprung from a very different attitude, namely that we were jealous that they had discovered a way of making quick money from which we were excluded. Jesus wept over Jerusalem, an expression of his great love for its people. We might also have wept, the tears springing from grief at the prospect of losing our business premises. This leads us to another guideline:

2. *Creative moods are to be distinguished from destructive by their effect. If the mood is leading to an increase of faith, hope and charity, then it is creative: if leading to a decrease of faith, hope and charity, then it is destructive.*

As soon as we become aware of our inner moods and feelings, we begin to know something of their complexity and how impossible it is to sift out clearly what is destructive from what is creative. The process of distinguishing can come only with practice. Our tendency will usually be to affix labels too quickly to our inner moods. We should allow them to teach us rather than assign them instantly to our 'good' and 'bad' mental filing-system. As we have already seen, painful moods and feelings may be destructive, but they can also be very creative, while moods and feelings which are very pleasant may be creative, but they can also be destructive. I can, for example, experience anger, sadness, anxiety which is, at a deeper level of my being, drawing me to God and making me more compassionate, tolerant of others, stronger in faith. In the technical language of spirituality, all those moods and inner feelings, which draw me to greater love of God and other people, are called 'consolation', whether the feeling be of peace, joy and delight or anger, sadness, anxiety. On other occasions we may experience anger, sadness and anxiety which enclose us more within ourselves, leading us into dark depths of self-sympathy, bitterness, resentment and alienation from ourselves, from everyone else and from God. In the technical language of spirituality, such feelings are called 'desolation' and they feel like it! So the third guideline is:

3. *Moods and inner feelings, whether painful or pleasant, which are drawing us towards God, are called 'consolation'. Painful moods and inner feelings which are drawing us away from God are called 'desolation'.*

Note that consolation can include both pleasant and painful inner states, while desolation includes only painful. Note, too, that desolation will only be experienced by those whose lives are essentially directed to the praise, reverence and service of God. If a person is turned away from God in the core of their being, they may experience the occasional sting of remorse, but in general the felt absence of God will not cause them any pain, just as a person who is ill and has lost all appetite is not pained at missing dinner. The fact that we experience desolation, although it feels like loss, is, in fact, a good sign, and so desolation as well as consolation is a sign of progress, not of regression, and it is an invitation to grow.

How are we to react when afflicted with desolation? The answer is in the fourth guideline:

4. *In desolation we should never go back on a decision made in time of consolation, because the thoughts and judgements which spring from desolation are the opposite of those which spring from consolation. It*

is, however, useful to act against the desolation, so that if it is leading us to pray less, we should pray more, and if it is leading us to be more enclosed on ourselves, we should go out more to others. We should also examine the cause of our desolation.

Desolation often follows close on the heels of consolation. We may glimpse something of the goodness, mercy, faithfulness of God and experience great peace and joy. The euphoria dies away and the mind begins to question, 'Was I under some kind of illusion?', 'I shall never be able to keep up a life of faith', 'What will my friends think of me?' The most common and pernicious form of desolation is lingering guilt, which we have already discussed on page 84. A quick way of spotting desolation is to ask yourself the question, 'Where is the focus of my attention? Is it on me, or is it on God?' Our subjective feelings are not bad or good in themselves. There is nothing wrong, for example, in our experiencing our own weakness, although this may feel very unpleasant, or in feeling that we are separated from God, out of touch with ourselves and with other people, unloving and unloved. Rightness and wrongness are applicable, not to these inner states, but only to our reactions to them. It is in the judgements and decisions which follow from these moods that we can act either creatively, by acting against the mood, or destructively, by going along with it. Feelings of separation from God and from others will tend to make us focus our attention on ourselves to the exclusion of God and others, producing gloomy thoughts of hopelessness and despair. In consolation, when we experience an increase of faith, hope and love, our attention will be more focussed on God's goodness, which will show up our sinfulness even more clearly, but in such a way that we shall know we are accepted by God, warts and all, giving hope and confidence.

Guideline number 4 is not saying that we should never make a decision in desolation, but is saying that we should not go back on decisions made in time of consolation. Desolation is a time for decisions which move us in the opposite direction from the movement of the desolation, therefore the importance of more prayer, more going out to others, etc. I have known many people who have made the most important decisions of their lives following on periods of desolation, because they acted against the desolation and spent time in examining its causes. Their decisions did not spring from the desolation itself, but from their opposing its movement by staying with the decisions they had made in consolation, opposing the movement of the desolation and examining its causes.

In examining the causes of desolation, one of the first questions we should ask is whether the mood is not caused by tiredness, physical or mental. God is a God of tenderness and compassion. If, instead of abandoning prayer when afflicted with desolation, we show our mood to God, he will teach us, so that we begin to know a time for resting and a time for working, a time for praying and a time for playing. If the desolation is not caused by tiredness, then resting or recreation will not change it and we must look for other causes.

Has desolation any connection with depression? This is an important and difficult question which it is well beyond my competence to answer, but I offer a few observations and very tentative conclusions based on limited experience of working with some people suffering from severe depression.

A depressed person who is also a Christian believer can suffer more severely than a non-believer if the depression so infects their minds and hearts that they become convinced that they are not only isolated from themselves and from others, but also from God, source of all hope. But if they can examine this awful pain, the pain itself can lead them to release from it. As a temporary measure, drugs may be necessary, but constant drug-taking can so muffle the inner feelings that the victim is cut off from their escape route.

Imaginative contemplation of Gospel healing miracles can reveal a root cause of depression in some believers. The revelation can be very painful, for the believer begins to see their own depth of unbelief and the false assumptions which have kept them enclosed in their depression, namely that their personal problems are not only greater than anyone else's, but that they are also beyond the power of God. Once a depressed person has acknowledged that God's power is always greater, and that there is no darkness or sense of guilt which he cannot overcome, the depression can begin to lift and cease to have such a complete hold.

Just as earlier we distinguished consolation and desolation, showing that consolation can be operative in painful as well as in pleasant feelings, so, too, I believe that consolation and desolation can be operative within a state of depression. My evidence for this statement is in personal experience, for I have known depression which moves towards God as well as depression which moves away from him. The distinction between the two states, both of them unpleasant, is in answer to the question, 'Where is this mood leading? Is it leading me to know God in the depths of my being as my only rock, refuge, strength, or is it leading me into a self-imprisoning preoccupation with my own darkness, a terrifying isolation which separates and encloses me within its faith-proof, hope-proof, love-proof walls?'

A further guideline for times of desolation:

5. *In desolation remember two things:*
i. Know that the desolation will pass.
ii. If you can keep the focus of your attention on God, even if you have no felt experience of his presence, he will teach you through the desolation. He is, as it were, gouging out your false securities, revealing himself to your own inner emptiness so that he may fill and possess it.

Desolation feels painful, but if we can be still during it, that is, not go back on decisions made in time of consolation, then the effect of the desolation, in itself tending to be destructive, becomes life-giving. If we imagine ourselves to be in the hands of God as clay is in the hands of the potter (an image used by Jeremiah and Isaiah), then we can see desolation as a turning of the clay so that it becomes a vessel which can contain life-giving water which as unformed clay it could not hold. Desolation, as it were, gouges us out, so that we can receive more. At the time, the process simply feels painful: when it is over we become aware of new areas of feeling and perception within us. Having experienced the inner pain, we can better sense it in others and we are much more appreciative of the gifts we have been given. We also discover in the pain deep strengths within, of which we were unaware before. We begin to understand in a new way the meaning of Christ, light of our darkness, and the meaning of his Passion, for he has come down into our pain, darkness and death, and is risen again. Therefore, there is no depth of experience I can reach where the rescuing power of God is not also present.

So far we have given guidelines for handling desolation. This sixth guideline is on handling consolation:

6. *In consolation, make the most of it! Acknowledge it as a gift, freely given, to reveal a deeper truth of your existence, namely, that you live always enfolded within the goodness and faithfulness of God. In consolation you have had a felt experience, a glimmer of this truth. Let this truth become the anchor of your hope in time of desolation.*

In experiencing feelings of peace, tranquillity, joy and delight – whether in prayer or outside of prayer – accept them gratefully from God. They are gifts given freely and through no merits of our own, which we should enjoy and relish. They are glimpses in our consciousness of the truth which permeates every particle of our being, that we live and move and have our being enfolded within the goodness of God. In a later chapter we shall look again at consolation and make further distinctions, but for the present accept any consolation gratefully and trust that if these feelings were arising from a destructive element within us, then God will eventually make it clear to us. The worst mistake we can make is to live in a state of constant suspicion that anything good that happens to us must be bad, or an illusion. Such distrust effectively chokes off the action of God as long as we persist in it. To live in him is to enjoy, as a normal state, love, joy, peace, patience, strength and trust.

One reason why most of us experience alternating consolation and desolation is because our minds have layers upon layers of consciousness. At one level of consciousness I may be full of faith that all power belongs to God and that without him I can do nothing. Then my security is threatened in some way and I reach a deeper level of consciousness to which my faith has not penetrated and where I have been living in a state of unconscious atheism. This moment of crisis is an invitation to grow in faith. I may accept the invitation and for a few years I live in this deeper level. Then another crisis occurs and I become aware of an even deeper level of atheism within me. In our journey towards God we proceed like those small birds whose flight is in loops. They always seem to be about to drop, but the drop in their flight seems to urge them forwards.

A constant theme running through this book is 'the answer is in the pain'. We fear whatever causes us pain and try to escape, but in escaping we are running away from the answer, and so another useful guideline in learning to read our moods is:

7. *Face the fears that haunt you.*

In Jungian language, 'Face your shadow.' Fear, like guilt, is a healthy human reaction to danger, but if we refuse to face the fear, we cannot discover the danger which is threatening. If we refuse to face the fear, the fear may become a ruthless tyrant pervading and poisoning every aspect of our lives. Once faced, the fears often turn out to be illusory, a truth vividly illustrated in a dream which someone shared with me while I was giving him the Spiritual Exercises. I shall call the dreamer 'Tom'.

It began as a nightmare. Tom was in a dark jungle, alone and unarmed, but there were threatening figures lurking in the shadows. He knew that the locality was called 'Recife', although at the time of the dream he had no idea where 'Recife' was. As he could not defend himself, he decided to try and befriend the threatening figures, some of whom vanished, while others proved friendly and protected him for the rest of his journey. Later, reflecting on the dream, he saw the pun on the word 'Recife', which was saying to him, ' "Receive" those things in your life of which you are afraid and befriend them.' He began to look at some of the fears in his life and discovered that some vanished, while others turned out to be sources of strength. One of the most constant refrains in the Old Testament and in the New is 'Do not be afraid'. God, in Christ, has overcome all the powers of evil and destruction. God is the God of surprises who can turn even the evil we have done, and the evil done to us, into the very means of our salvation. The Church at Easter sings a beautiful poem which begins with the Latin word 'Exsultet', meaning 'Rejoice', and includes the phrase, 'O felix culpa', meaning 'O happy fault', and goes on to give the reason, 'O necessary sin of Adam, which gained for us so great a Redeemer'.

A very good way of facing our fears is to reveal them to someone we can trust who will listen and will accept us as we are. Having put the fear into words and given it a name, it no longer has such power over us, a truth exemplified daily and nightly in the work of the Samaritans, a voluntary organization which invites people in distress and who are feeling suicidal to ring up at any time and talk to someone.

I am aware that this chapter may not have been easy reading! I conclude with a caution. Let consolation and desolation announce their own arrival and do not indulge in narcissistic preoccupation with your inner moods. It is characteristic of both consolation and desolation that they usually take us by surprise, because they are reactions arising within us which are beyond the immediate grasp of our conscious minds. Often, too, we are not immediately aware of what is happening within us, and we only recognize the mood of consolation/desolation later. A good example of this truth is in St Luke's account of the two disciples walking to Emmaus. While they are walking with the stranger, they do not seem to be aware of anything extraordinary, being too absorbed in their own feelings of loss. Later, when they have recognized Jesus in the breaking of bread, they say to each other 'Did not our hearts burn within us as he talked to us on the road?' At first, be content to spot the more obvious experiences of consolation or desolation and do not be surprised if they seem infrequent. With practice, you will be able to spot the quality of your inner moods more quickly.

Christ welcomed sinners and dined with them. He welcomes us and makes his home in us. Our home can never be the same again. He can prove to be an awkward guest who tends to take over everything, invading our privacy, disrupting our plans. He can upset our relationships, introduces unwanted people and disturbing ideas, puts our property, our jobs and even our lives at risk. We do not dare ask him to leave, but we can relegate him to a small corner of the house which can be securely locked, soothe our consciences by decorating this corner tastefully, sparing no expense, bowing or genuflecting reverently when we pass by, and then get on with normal living, happy to claim him as a guest while ensuring that he does not interfere, reducing him to a nice, domesticated, comforting, harmless Jesus.

The next chapter illustrates this tendency, which is in all of us, to domesticate Christ.

Exercises

(Do not be surprised if, at first, you find it difficult to grasp these Rules for Discernment. The following exercises may help you to recognize these rules in your own experience.)

1. Can you, by reviewing your own experience, identify any moods or inner feelings which you would call consolation or desolation?

2. Can you find within your own experience any examples of Rule 4 (page 96), Rule 6 (page 100) or Rule 7 (page 101)?

3. Try writing your own Rules for Discernment based on your own experience.

9

A Most Surprising God

Tantum Religio potuit suadere malorum.
Such evil deeds can religion prompt.   (Lucretius)

In France and Germany there are vast cemeteries containing
the mortal remains of those hundreds of thousands of men
who died in battle in the two World Wars. Both German and
Allied graveyards declare that their dead gave their lives 'Pro
Deo et Patria', 'For God and Country'. All who gave their
lives deserve our respect, but it cannot be God's will that we
should kill one another. Nuclear submarines, built for
national security and therefore 'Pro Patria', with enough fire
power to obliterate cities and maim millions, have received
solemn blessings to assure those who sail in them and operate
their missiles that they act 'Pro Deo' as well as 'Pro Patria'.
Sin is the refusal to let God be God. This refusal is so deep
in us that we even use God's name to justify our selfishness,
oppression and destruction and believe that we are acting
righteously.

In the last chapter we looked at some basic guidelines to
help us distinguish the creative action of God in our lives
from the destructive action of evil within us. In this and the
following chapters we shall look more closely at this question.

Christ died, rose from the dead and is now Lord of all
creation. Our real identity is in him. 'The Spirit of God', St
Paul says, 'who lived in Jesus and raised him from the dead,
now lives in us,' and so he prays for the Ephesians,

> Out of his infinite glory, may he give you the power through
> his Spirit for your hidden self to grow strong, so that Christ
> may live in your hearts through faith, and then, planted in
> love and built on love, you will with all the saints have

strength to grasp the breadth and the length, the height and the depth; until, knowing the love of Christ, which is beyond all knowledge, you are filled with the utter fullness of God. (Eph. 3:16–19)

Each one of us 'This one work has to do, Let all God's glory through.' But we are all tempted to take God over, 'to be as gods', and to use Christ to justify our own greed, timidity and self-righteousness.

If Christ were to appear in the flesh today, how would we receive him? The rest of this chapter is an imaginative exercise in answer to this question. Although it is written as a bit of light relief after the last heavy chapter, it has a serious purpose, namely to help us see some of the subtle ways in which our 'common sense', respectability and religious conditioning may blind us to the truth of Christ, so that we fail to recognize him living and loving in the men and women of our day. Particular embellishments of the Gospel story included in this exercise are not to be taken seriously. I do not, for example, believe that all bookstalls should be banned from the back of churches! Having read the chapter, I hope you can then take the idea and do some writing of your own on Jesus of the Gospel and his likely reception in your church today.

I imagine that I am a parish priest in Northern Ireland, the place chosen because it reflects something of the fierce religious and political conflicts which divided Palestine in the time of Christ. The parish priest is exasperated by the behaviour of a man in his parish, who has applied to seminaries and religious houses in the U.K. for admission as a candidate for the priesthood. Bishops, and religious superiors from England, Scotland and Wales are now writing to the parish priest asking for a reference for the candidate. The overworked parish priest has been sending a brief reply, declaring the man to be totally unsuited for acceptance. Many have written again asking for a fuller reference. In reply, the parish priest sends out the following circular:

The Presbytery, The Square,
Portinstorm, Co. Trim.

To Their Excellencies, Graces, Lordships,
Lord Abbots, Very Reverend Provincials
of England, Wales and Scotland.

Reverend and Dear Brothers in Christ,

Please forgive me for sending you a circular letter, but I do so in the hope that the few minutes required for its perusal may save Your Reverences time, money and the possible disruption of your seminaries and noviceships.

A young man, Mr E. Manuel, aged 33, and of this parish, has already applied to some of you and may well apply to the rest, for acceptance into your diocese, religious order or congregation. Some of you have asked me to supply a reference. I have replied simply stating that I do not consider him a suitable applicant, as charity and overwork compelled me to be brief. A few of you have asked for a more detailed report. While I appreciate Your Reverences' desire to be fair to this man and to nurture any sign of a priestly vocation, however unlikely, in these times of distressing shortage, I do not, unfortunately, have the leisure for letter writing of the unemployed Mr Manuel. In addition to my heavy parish duties, I have also been asked by His Lordship the Bishop to take over the diocesan marriage tribunal in succession to Mgr Colquhoun, who suffered a coronary two years ago following on a meeting with the same Mr Manuel. I am also without a housekeeper for reasons which I shall explain later.

My personal knowledge of Mr Manuel is limited to a few brief encounters. When I first came to this parish three years ago, Mr Manuel had already left home and he returns only spasmodically, D.G. However, I have spoken at length with people who do know him well, and in particular with the new parish accountant, a bright and ambitious young man, who at one time associated with Mr Manuel.

Manuel's parents (his father died some years ago) first came to the parish over twenty-five years ago. Some say that they had been travelling people, a rumour made the more credible by the subsequent vagrancy of their son, and by his mother, a singularly silent woman, a characteristic not uncommon among gypsies who are no longer on the road.

Those closest to the family maintain that the deceased Mr Manuel was not, in fact, the father of the child. I am still old-fashioned enough to believe that such facts can be important.

In his early teens, E. Manuel disappeared while on holiday with his parents and was missing for three days. It is, as Your Reverences are no doubt aware, a well known fact that truancy at an early age frequently betokens mental imbalance. On being recovered and questioned, the child maintained that he had been attending to his father's affairs. This could, of course, be explained by his illegitimate birth, which he may have discovered; but some of the relatives have a more sinister interpretation and are convinced he is possessed.

He has no formal education to speak of and was apprenticed to his father, a joiner, at an early age. As a youth he was given to wandering on his own, was strangely silent much of the time, but is also gifted with a fatal fluency and charm of manner, which can easily deceive the unwary, of whom we have more than a fair proportion in this part of the world. Three years ago he gave up his job and took to the road, returning occasionally, sometimes alone, but more often with an unsavoury group of companions who include, besides a few simple-minded folk, some notorious men of violence, extortioners and prostitutes. Again, it is a well established fact that a man can be judged by the friends he keeps. Currently there is a court case pending in which a local farmer is suing Mr Manuel and a local lunatic for the joint destruction of a large herd of pigs. They evidently chased the pigs over a cliff into the sea.

Without formal education in either the sacred or secular sciences, Manuel has set himself up as a religious preacher, making theological assertions about himself and God which would cause alarm even on the western seaboard of the U.S.A.

In the foolishly permissive spirit which has infected some sections of the Church in the last twenty years, a joint meeting of the U.C.M. (Union of Catholic Mothers) and the Knights of St Columba, seeing the influence which Mr Manuel was exercising in some sections of the community, invited him to address them. His address was a salutary warning against such permissiveness, for he assured the assembly that the criminals and prostitutes would enter the kingdom of heaven before them.

An over-tolerant parish council also invited him to speak, and he was lucky to escape with his life at the end of it. His provocative remarks, suggesting that Protestants and pagans were nearer to God than they were, caused uproar and a very unpleasant scene. I leave it to Your Reverences to judge for yourselves which kind of spirit there must be in a man who can cause such anger and uproar when addressing religiously minded people.

When I first came to the parish, having heard stories of Mr Manuel's doings and wanting to judge for myself, I invited him, but without his companions, to meet some of the local clergy for supper, including Mgr Colquhoun, our leading moralist and president of the diocesan marriage tribunal. On arrival, Mr Manuel was treated with appropriate courtesy by the assembled clergy. Supper had hardly begun when a woman of notorious reputation in the town entered the dining room without as much as a 'by your leave' and proceeded to display her affection in a thoroughly distasteful display of sentimentality and hysteria. The assembled company, as Your Reverences might well imagine, sat in stunned silence. Manuel then had the impertinence to address me, comparing unfavourably the formal welcome which we, the clergy, accorded with the lady's tearful effusions. He then had the temerity to assure the woman that her sins were forgiven because she believed in him! It was at this point that Mgr Colquhoun departed and later suffered a heart attack. As a result of this gesture of friendliness towards Manuel, I have not only had to take over Mgr Colquhoun's heavy responsibilities, but I have also lost my housekeeper, who, scandalized by the incident, could not be persuaded that I had not invited the lady personally to supper, an invitation never accorded to herself in twenty years' devoted service.

Manuel preaches to the people in the open air, occasionally providing picnics. Although unemployed, he seems able to command limitless quantities of food and, on one occasion at least, drink, too, which he dispenses liberally, so that his meetings are more in the nature of parties rather than religious services. On one occasion he had the impertinence to offer the presbytery some of the food left over. Unable to believe the food was not stolen property, I passed it on to the Salvation Army as an ecumenical gesture, having first consulted the diocesan moralist.

In his preaching, his fatal fluency and ability to turn a telling phrase does untold damage to the minds of the simple faithful, undermining their religious and moral life, as well as their respect for the authority of the clergy. Although Mr Manuel claims that he has never preached disobedience to the authority of the Church, he can hardly expect the simple faithful to obey with reverence those whom he has labelled 'a brood of vipers' and 'whited sepulchres'. He refers to Almighty God as 'Dad', a Dad who apparently spends his time pursuing the likes of Manuels' friends, the criminals and prostitutes. He also implies that the Sunday obligation is for the benefit of the people rather than to fulfil the prescriptions of law, and he has effected a notable drop in Sunday observance throughout the country.

Politically, in the violent, complicated and delicate situation in which we live, he is bewilderingly naive. He seems to have no understanding of the need for cohesion in the Catholic body if we are to preserve our corporate strength in this trouble-torn land. His so-called teaching ignores the very real differences which separate the Christian denominations in this part of the country, diverts peoples' attention from the hard facts of moral theology and prescriptions of the magisterium, concentrating their attention instead on 'Dad', who seems to love everyone with the possible exception of those of us who are responsible for preaching, teaching and sanctifying the Church!

He claims to have no political affiliations and denounces all forms of violence, whether it be the British army, the I.R.A., or the U.D.A., yet his teaching on 'Dad', far from bringing peace, intensifies the divisions because he threatens every faction. Some suspect that he may, in spite of his protestations, harbour political ambitions, for he is known to meet secretly with some prominent members in every party, a fact which, when it becomes public, will certainly endanger his own and other peoples' lives. In our delicate political situation, where rash and imprudent words can be as damaging as bombs, Mr Manuel is like a walking arsenal.

Like so many people who claim to work for peace, E.

Manuel is himself of violent temperament. Just recently he created a scene outside the Cathedral, overthrowing the repository and bookstall tables. The matter was, of course, reported to the police and there is a warrant out for his arrest, but he has disappeared for the time being.

Most disturbing of all is the belief that he may, in fact, be possessed. Some of his own relatives do not hesitate to assert this. He has certainly had association with possessed people, both men and women, some of whom are now his permanent followers. He also seems to have some kind of preternatural powers not uncommon among the possessed.

It may be that he will be caught and arrested shortly and there are enough charges against him to keep him out of harm's way for a long time to come, but he has a serpentlike cunning and may well escape the country to continue his troublemaking elsewhere.

I apologize again to Your Reverences for the length of this letter but, had I not written, some of you, in the present widespread shortage of vocations to the priesthood, might have wasted time and money in encouraging this man, who can seem so plausible at first, but who would have a devastating effect on any seminary or religious house imprudent enough to accept him.

Begging a remembrance in Your Reverences' prayers and assuring you of my own for an increase in worthy vocations to your diocese, order, congregation,

I remain,
Yours sincerely,
(P. Simon, DD, Parish Priest of Portinstorm)

While writing this letter and entering into some of the blind spots of P. Simon, I began to recognize a few more of my own.

Because we are all liable to self-deception and tend to use God and Christ to justify and support our own narrow ways of thinking and acting, we need the institutional and the critical elements of the Church as a check to our self-deception, but ultimately it is Christ himself who is our teacher. Christ is mystery. We can never possess the truth of Christ: all we can do is beg to be possessed by him, his truth and his love 'which is beyond all knowledge'. Imaginative contemplation on scenes from the Gospel is an invaluable way of coming to recognize Christ today living in our hearts. When he makes his home in us, it is not that we let Jesus into our lives, but rather we surrender our home to him, for he is Lord of all, who loves all that he has created.

The next two chapters offer a few reflections on the life, death and resurrection of Christ, intended to encourage the reader to contemplate Christ of the Gospels imaginatively so that you can meet him in your own way, which is the best and only way for you!

Exercise

Read one of the Gospels carefully and then write either a letter, article, or short story describing Christ living today, how and by whom he would be welcomed, how and by whom he is likely to be rejected.

10

Knowing Christ

For him I have accepted the loss of everything, and I look on everything as so much rubbish if only I can have Christ and be given a place in him. (Phil. 3:8–9)

When people begin to use their imagination on Gospel scenes, they are often surprised at the Christ they meet. To some he seems much more ordinary than they would have expected, others are surprised, or even shocked by the Christ they find, like the man who saw a Christ playing the clown and doing cartwheels. Surprise can be a sign that we are encountering the living Christ, image of the God of surprises. St John writes, 'He came to his own, but his own did not accept him' (John 1:11), because he did not match their expectations of a glorious and powerful messiah. The problem continues: in Christian teaching we have so emphasized the divinity of Christ that his humanity is obscured and so we fail to recognize him in our own or in other peoples'. The Church has always taught that Christ is perfectly human as well as divine and that his divinity in no way lessens but, on the contrary, perfects his humanity.

So the first guideline for reading/contemplating the Gospel is *to see Christ as a human being*, limited, constricted, who had to learn who God is, had to grow in faith all through his life, experienced human emotions of love and joy, fear and dread, had likes and dislikes, suffered hunger, thirst and weariness, and was tempted. It is only in and through his humanity, and the experience of our own and other peoples', that we can begin to know the meaning of his divinity. He meets us where we are, in our humanity, and not outside it, and reveals himself most intimately as a presence in our emptiness, a

112

companion living within the core of our loneliness. Our humanity is precious: it is what God could become. This leads us to a second guideline:

Whenever and whatever we read of Christ in the Gospel, we are also reading our own self-portrait, for Christ is what we are called to become. 'God became man' as one of the early Fathers of the Church put it, 'so that man might become God.' Christ is not simply, nor primarily, a model of good behaviour whom we must imitate. He is the source of our life and the sense of it, for to be another Christ is the meaning of our existence. 'The Spirit of him who raised Jesus from the dead is living in you' (Rom. 8:11). By looking at him in the Gospel scenes we begin to catch glimpses of what God has called us to become before the world was, namely, other Christs.

The third guideline forms the rest of this chapter and is an attempt to find the key to Christ's personality. Resuming the analogy with which the book began, the field within which the treasure is hidden is our own life and the treasure is our inner self, our Christ self. The Church, through the Scripture first of all, and through its own understanding of the Scripture, points us to Christ, but her role is like that of the person who tells us where to dig in the field, then shows us the safe containing the treasure. As the treasure is within our inner self, to which we alone have access, neither the Church nor anyone within the Church can open the treasure for us. It is as though we each have our own bank card number, which only Christ can teach us. That is why prayer is not an optional extra for the more devout Christian, but is of the essence of Christian life. Without prayer in the Church, without an emphasis on the mystical element, we become like misers, fiercely jealous of our treasure box, content to possess it but without ever enjoying it. The contents could be full of old bones or crawling with worms. We guard it, treasure it, defend it by fair means or foul, not because we have any personal appreciation of its contents, but because we have been conditioned to believe that our lives depend on our guarding this treasure box, but we have never been told, or have never felt the need, to examine its contents. This attitude is the root cause of division within the Church and between the Churches. Christ becomes a label which we stick on the nonsense of our own lives, on our greed and power lust, on the cult of our comfort and self-importance. When challenged or criticized, we wave our Christ label in front of our opponents, declare them unorthodox, heretical and a threat to our eternal destiny, threatening and, if we consider it necessary for our own and God's defence, murdering them. The real divisions in the Church today are not divisions between Christian denominations but between those Christians who have opened the treasure and live with the life it provides, and those Christians who are still sitting on closed boxes, alarmed and afraid, and condemning those who show signs of a new life in Christ.

This third guideline cannot open the treasure for us but it can preserve us from the danger of worshipping idols of our own manufacture to which we affix the label 'Christ'. The guideline is Christ's relationship to his Father, for it is this relationship which gives unity and coherence to his life and teaching and therefore gives unity and coherence to our lives, too.

The only words recorded in the Gospels as spoken by Christ in the first thirty years of his life are in Luke's account of Jesus' meeting with his parents after they had lost him for three days, 'Did you not know that I must be busy with my Father's affairs?' (Luke 2:49). Among his last phrases are: 'Father, if you are willing, take this cup away from me. Nevertheless, let your will be done, not mine' (Luke 26:42), and when dying on the cross, ' "Father, into your hands I commit my spirit." With these words he breathed his last' (Luke 23:46). The first words of Christ recorded by Mark are: 'The kingdom of God is close at hand' – and 'the kingdom' means the reign of his Father.

Christ's perception of his world, the way he acts and reacts, the teaching he gives, all is permeated with his relationship to his Father. Knowledge of his Father pervades his being as yeast affects the whole loaf, as salt gives relish to food, as light penetrates darkness. Whatever his eyes see, whether it be the sparrows, lilies of the field, the crops being sown or harvested, the sheep being shepherded, the fruit on trees, the landscape, the colour and shape of clouds, the features of men's faces, their dress, social conventions, the world of economics or of politics, he sees it all in relation to his Father.

How does Jesus see his Father? We can begin to answer

by looking at the parables he uses, because the parables reveal his ways of looking and assessing.

One of Jesus' favourite images of the kingdom, in which his Father is king, is of a banquet, a marriage feast. When those originally invited refuse to come, the king sends his servants to scour the streets and invite everyone they can find 'good and bad alike'. In Luke's gospel the servants bring in the poor, the crippled, the blind and the lame. The king is still not satisfied: 'Go to the open roads and hedgerows and force people to come in to make sure my house is full.'

The Father is presented as a God of overflowing goodness, whose one desire is to share whatever he has with as many as possible. The only people who incur his anger, as he is described in the parables, are those who refuse to accept his goodness or who prevent other people from doing so.

In the parable of the Two Sons, the Father is represented as foolishly lavish toward the prodigal son, even more prodigal than the boy! He would have shown admirable generosity if he had accepted his son home again after disgracing the family; to watch for the son's return, to rush out as soon as he comes in sight, to embrace, clothe with sandals, a cloak, a ring and then to kill the prize calf and throw a party is all a bit excessive, and our prudent, measured and well-controlled selves, brought-up on Aristotle's 'Virtue lies in the mean between extremes', can have every sympathy with the sober-minded, hard-working elder brother. Faced with his elder son's indignation, the Father remains his lavish self, telling him 'all I have is yours'.

There is a foolish prodigality, too, in the Father who is presented as leaving the ninety-nine sheep to go and hunt for the one that is lost, a foolishness which we so often correct in the Church by concentrating our attention and energies on the one which is safe and leaving the ninety-nine!

The Father is also represented as financially imprudent, forgiving the debtor who owes ten thousand talents, a fortune of many millions of pounds in our terms, without a qualm, but getting into a rage with that same debtor when he tried to squeeze a paltry sum from someone else. The wrath of the Father is reserved for the mean and the stingy, like this extortionate debtor, or like Dives who feasts richly while Lazarus starves at his gate. The Father is pictured as so careless about money that he could be accused of conniving at dishonesty, as in the parable of the unjust steward who, knowing he is in trouble and to secure some friends, fiddles the accounts in favour of the king's debtors; the king commends him for his dishonesty! He pays last-minute workers as much as full-day workers and seems opposed to prudence in money matters. The careful steward who kept his talent safe and intact for his master's return is condemned: the other two stewards who took risks and produced more talents are praised.

In the parables, the Father is presented as lavish, prodigal and somewhat foolish by our standards. His value system would not get him very far in this world! His expression in human terms, his Word, Jesus, shows the same lavish characteristics as the Father. At Cana, he produces an unnecessarily large quantity of wine, 180 gallons, and of unnecessarily high quality for the tail end of a feast. When he feeds the five thousand, there are twelve full baskets left over. His carelessness in money matters is criminal and contributed to his final downfall after he had thrown over the money-changers' tables and driven them from the Temple.

Because he is at one with his Father, therefore Christ is no respecter of persons and does not need the support of rank or status. His own description of himself as 'the Son of Man' is, according to some commentators, the translation of Aramaic slang for 'an ordinary bloke', or in Scottish terminology 'an ordinary punter'. His being, as man, is the reflection of God's own being and therefore, although in himself he is best described as 'for the Father', to us he appears as 'the man for others', for it is the nature of God to be for us. This essential characteristic of Christ is expressed most vividly in the accounts of the Last Supper. Christ, one with the Father,

> . . . knew that the Father had put everything into his hands, and that he had come from God and was returning to God, and he got up from table, removed his outer garment and, taking a towel, wrapped it round his waist; he then poured water into a basin and began to wash the disciples' feet and to wipe them with the towel he was wearing. (John 13:2ff.)

This is the action of God translated into human terms, the

God who washes feet! In this action, Christ is not just giving an example of service: he is communicating the very life of God. 'If I do not wash you,' he says to the protesting Peter, 'you can have nothing in common with me.' But the life of God is given to us, as it was given to Christ, for the life of others, and so Christ tells his friends, 'If I, then, the Lord and Master, have washed your feet, you should wash each other's feet' (13:14–15).

In the other Gospel accounts of the Last Supper, Christ takes the bread, blesses and breaks it, saying, 'Take and eat: this is me given for you. Do this in my memory.' The life of the Father, expressed in the human Jesus, is a life that is given for us – 'All I have is yours.' 'Do this in memory' is not an instruction to perform a ritual, but a request to let the life of Christ, and therefore of the Father, a life of sharing, become our life.

As the life of Christ takes hold on us, our lives will be transformed from being lives of self-protection, self-care, self-cultivation, into lives given for others, because God, the God of compassion, will have taken possession of our being. When Jesus describes the Final Judgement, the saved are those who lived the compassion of God, 'I was hungry and you gave me to eat, thirsty and you gave me drink, . . .' (Matt. 25), and the lost are those without compassion: 'I tell you solemnly, in so far as you neglected to do this to one of the least of these, you neglected to do it to me.'

The wrath of God is reserved for those who refuse compassion, no matter how religiously observant and religiously scrupulous they may be.

> I hate and despise your feasts, I take no pleasure in your solemn festivals. When you offer me holocausts, I reject your oblations . . . Let me have no more of the din of your chanting, no more of your strumming on harps. But let justice flow like water, and integrity like an unfailing stream. (Amos 5:21–5)

And St Paul has harsh words for those who look to religious observance for their salvation:

> If you have really died with Christ to the principles of this world, why do you still let rules dictate to you, as though

117

you were still living in the world? It is forbidden to pick up this, it is forbidden to taste that, it is forbidden to touch something else; all these prohibitions are only concerned with things that perish by their very use – an example of human doctrines and regulations! It may be argued that true wisdom is to be found in these, with their self-imposed devotions, their self-abasement, and their severe treatment of the body; but once the flesh starts to protest, they are no use at all. (Col. 2:20–3).

'The flesh', in St Paul's writings, means all those areas of our being which resist God. Paul before his conversion, living a life of strict observance of the law and therefore of great asceticism, would have later described himself as having lived a 'life of the flesh'.

Jesus of the Gospel is the most gentle of men, full of understanding and compassion, but he is also the most intransigent. 'You cannot serve God and Mammon' (Luke 16:13). 'He who is not with me is against me' (Matt. 12:30). In Christian tradition life is seen as a warfare between the forces of good and evil, between God and Mammon, a warfare in which we are all involved, whether we like it or not, and in which there is no neutrality. The life of God is a life of giving, a life for others: the life of Mammon is the opposite, a life of self-preservation at the expense of others. In Christian tradition the spirit of Mammon, the false god, is personified in the Devil or Satan, also called Lucifer, meaning the light-bearer, because he presents himself under the appearance of light, is specious and plausible, but the 'Father of lies' as St John calls him.

In his Spiritual Exercises, before beginning to contemplate Christ in his public life, Ignatius gives a 'Meditation on the Two Standards' which he considers so important that he asks the person doing the Exercises to spend a whole day on this one meditation, doing it once for an hour and then going over the same meditation for another three separate hours. The Standards are the Standard of Satan and the Standard of Christ, proposed not as a choice, for he presumes the retreatant has chosen the Standard of Christ, but in order to make us more aware of the subtle ways in which, under the appearance of good, Lucifer, whom Ignatius also calls 'the enemy of our human nature', works his destruction on the world.

The reader may dislike this Devil/Satan/Lucifer terminology. If so, ignore it, but what we cannot ignore is the terrifying destructiveness which can infect and possess the human spirit. It can enter politely, plausibly, respectably, even religiously, germinate quietly and peacefully for a while, then erupt in savagery and destruction.

A few years ago, on a beautiful day in May, I walked by the Holy Loch in Scotland, where the Polaris submarines are based. The waters were still, reflecting the hills and sky, their surface ruffled only slightly by the periscope of a nuclear submarine passing smoothly beneath the surface. This scene reflected the reality in which we all live, the reality both outside and within us. On the surface everything seemed beautiful and orderly: beneath the surface were powers of destruction which can consume whole populations in a ball of fire, scorch, torture and maim those who survive, and continue to do so in generations yet unborn.

In his 'Two Standards' meditation, Ignatius gives an image of evil, picturing Lucifer sitting on a smoky throne in the plain of Babylon and surrounded by little demons whom he sends throughout the world 'so that no Province, no place, no state of life, no individual is overlooked'.

The little demons are instructed to ensnare all human beings in three stages: to teach them to covet riches, so leading them on to love the honours of this world until they are trapped in the prison of their pride.

Riches, in themselves, are not evil, nor are honours, position in society and status. In themselves these things are good and can be used for the praise, reverence and service of God, but riches are for sharing, not for hoarding, and honour and power is for greater service of others, not to enhance a false sense of self-importance. Riches and honour can become our idols, our Mammon, so that our lives revolve around our bank balance, whether its abundance or deficit, or around the esteem, or lack of it, in which we imagine we are held.

As individuals, as a Church, and as a nation we need to ponder the truth in this representation of Satan's Standard and why he is called 'the enemy of our human nature'. The riches of the earth are a blessing. Destructiveness enters when they become an idol, so that we value ourselves and other people not for their intrinsic worth, but for their market value. We are all worthy of honour, far more worthy than we think. It is not riches and honour which are wrong, but the way we use them. We fail to honour one another because we do not value and cherish one another for what we are in ourselves, images of God, but we value people for the wealth they possess, the power they can exercise. Consequently, those who have neither riches nor honour are devalued, considered worthless and, unless they have great inner strength, come to look on themselves as worthless. There is a high suicide rate among the unemployed of Britain today. The rich pride themselves on their wealth and the powerful take delight in their status, which is to devalue their own real worth. As individuals and as a nation we can become so enamoured of our riches and our prestige that we cling to them as to life itself, will go to any lengths to secure them, even to mass murder and the risk of annihilation. The spirit of evil is rightly called 'the father of lies' and 'the enemy of our human nature'.

'Mammon' and riches mean not only money and material possessions, but stand for any idol in our lives, any created thing which becomes the focus of our praise, reverence and service. Mammon can be an ideology or any 'ism' which we allow to possess us. Mammon can be patriotism, my country right or wrong, or it can be the way in which we practise religion, when our dedication becomes dedication to particular structures or formulations of the Christian message, and their preservation in the form familiar to us becomes more important than the worship and service of God, the God of mystery and of love, before whom all human structures must be provisional. 'The Sabbath is made for man, not man for the Sabbath,' as Jesus said to the Pharisees.

In the 'Two Standards' meditation, in contrast to Satan on his smoky throne, Ignatius pictures Christ standing in a plain near Jerusalem with his friends around him, 'his appearance beautiful and attractive'. Unless we see Christ and his teaching as attractive, as the answer to our deepest desires, we shall never follow him wholeheartedly. It is only in the strength of our attachment to him that we shall become detached, indifferent to riches and honour.

As Satan is pictured sending the little demons all over the

world, Ignatius pictures Christ sending his friends to all human beings, 'no matter what their state or condition', a phrase reminiscent of the wedding feast parable in which the king sends the servants to the hedgerows and byways to invite everyone they can find, good and bad alike. They are to help all people by attracting them first to the highest spiritual poverty, and even to actual poverty, if that is what God is asking of them, and secondly to accept and even desire the insults and contempt of the world, because this will lead them to humility, the source of all other virtues.

At a first reading, Christ's programme of poverty, insults and contempt leading to humility, sounds most unattractive. Spiritual poverty means a mind and heart which so trusts in God as its rock, refuge and strength that nothing in creation can deflect from God. Spiritual poverty is a phrase which describes one aspect of Christ's relationship to the Father, namely that he was so anchored and rooted in the life of his Father that nothing could possess him, neither his desire to have ('Turn these stones into bread'), nor his desire to count and be important ('Leap down from the pinnacle of the Temple'), nor the desire to have power ('Take over the kingdoms of the world'). St Paul expresses his own poverty of spirit in these words to the Philippians, 'I know how to be poor and I know how to be rich too. I have been through my initiation and now I am ready for anything anywhere: full stomach or empty stomach, poverty or plenty. There is nothing I cannot master with the help of the One who gives me strength' (4:12–13).

Spiritual poverty is the opposite of diffidence, timidity, self-depreciation, crawling servility. It is the possession of all things in Christ, while being possessed by none, the ability to enjoy and delight in God's creation without being trapped by it, it is the discovery of our true identity, that we live in, through and with Christ in the life of the Father. Spiritual poverty is spiritual freedom.

'Blessed are the poor in spirit; theirs is the kingdom of heaven' (Matt. 5:3). This, the first of the beatitudes, is a summary of the whole of Christ's sermon on the mount, the essence of his teaching.

Actual poverty, if understood as material deprivation imposed on people against their will, is not a good, but an evil, and therefore to be opposed and overcome. The riches of this world are for the benefit of all human beings. The material deprivation of half the world is not because there is not enough food and resources, but because of their unjust distribution. A Christian who is not striving to be spiritually poor has ceased to be a Christian. It is of the nature of spiritual poverty, because it is the attitude which allows God's goodness, generosity and compassion to act in us, to combat material deprivation and oppose all that contributes to it, whether it be our own individual selfishness and greed, or our corporate selfishness and greed expressed in our political and economic systems.

Some individuals are called to renounce all legal right to material possessions as a sign of their complete trust in God. All members of religious orders and of most religious congregations take vows of actual poverty so that the individual members have no right to personal possessions, but whatever they have is held in common. The problem is that common ownership often gives individual Religious a material security which only the wealthy individual can enjoy! However, those vowed to actual poverty should be the most effective people in working for the alleviation of material deprivation. If they are not the most effective, then it is a sign that the actual poverty they profess is no longer an expression of spiritual poverty and therefore that they are no longer living as channels of God's goodness, generosity and compassion.

Many Christians feel called to experience actual poverty in the sense of material deprivation, not because it is good in itself, but because they want to be at one with Christ in the materially poor. Material poverty, voluntarily undertaken, draws them more deeply into the life of Christ who chose to be poor. In this poverty we discover new values and new joys within ourselves and others which no one can take away from us, because our being is becoming a sharing and so we are living more in the life of God. In today's world of gross injustice and oppression of the poor, every Christian is called to grow in this kind of poverty. That is why the Roman Catholic and many other Churches have pledged themselves in all their work and ministry to make the poor, not the powerful and influential, their primary concern.

It is relatively easy to be detached from material

possessions. It is much more difficult to be spiritually poor in relation to what Ignatius calls 'honours', which include everything that can contribute to a false sense of self-importance: our popularity, status in society, our physical health, strength, beauty, our intelligence, qualifications, achievements, our ideas, including our ideas about God and spirituality. An indication of the tenacity with which we cling to honours can be measured by the hurt we feel when all that 'honour' stands for is impugned. We feel crushed when overlooked or not appreciated because our deepest securities are being attacked and our whole self-preservation instinct rallies all our forces to repel this attack on what we suppose to be our inmost being. What we are defending is not, in fact, ourselves, but our own false notion of our own worth and meaning.

If love of material possessions, the desire to have, is compared to the walls of the tomb we construct for ourselves, love of our own self-importance may be compared to hard scales which grow from our skin, encasing us firmly in its armour-like plating. While it is relatively painless to knock down the walls of our tomb, removing the scales is like scalping, a very painful operation. A very good indication of whether and where we are encased in such scales is to ask ourselves the question, 'What events in life disturb me most?' If we can locate the pain, we may be able to discover its source.

If I have poverty of spirit, I can afford to listen carefully and with interest to personal criticisms from others. Perhaps I have to acknowledge that I am incompetent in my job, that I have a prickly temperament, that I am not very intelligent, sensitive, strong, beautiful in comparison with the people around me. I am judging and assessing myself through comparisons with other people. If God is my rock, my refuge and my strength then I have no need to be defensive, for I know he accepts me as I am and that I am precious in his eyes, that his power is greatest in my weakness and that it is through my weakness that I come to a knowledge of my true identity and worth, called before the world was, to be at one with him in whom all things exist. St Catherine of Genoa once said, 'We can truly know by continual experience that the love of God is our repose, our joy, our life, and that false self-love is but a constant weariness, sadness and a living death of our true selves,' which re-echoes the cry of delight of Mary: 'My soul proclaims the greatness of the Lord and my spirit exults in God my saviour; because he has looked upon his lowly handmaid' (Luke 1:47).

Spiritual poverty leads to humility, an interesting word derived from the Latin, 'humus', meaning 'the earth'. Humility means recognizing our creaturehood, having a true sense of perspective, knowing our worth as dwelling places of God. Humility is freedom from every form of inner enslavement, is the ability to laugh and delight in God's creation as well as to feel its pain. It is the opposite of crawling servility, self-diffidence, self-hate and infantile docility.

This, then, is the third guideline for all our reading and contemplating the Christ of the Gospels – *that prayer for Christ's poverty of spirit should always be included*, for as he grants us poverty of spirit, so we open the treasure that is in us.

'The kingdom of heaven is like a mustard seed which a man took and sowed in his field' (Matt. 13:31). The growth of the kingdom within our hearts is slow. What is important is not the present size of the mustard seed within us, but that we allow it to germinate. In other words, keep praying for poverty of spirit and do not be deterred by what you consider your poor progress. Preoccupation with our spiritual progress is unhealthy, a sign of our false self. We must accept our failures, whether they be real or imagined, as opportunities for growth in knowledge of the truth that God, and God alone, is our rock, our refuge and our strength. St Paul writes of the joy of this truth: 'For I am certain of this: neither death nor life, no angel, no prince, nothing that exists, nothing still to come, not any power, or height or depth, nor any created thing, can ever come between us and the love of God made visible in Christ Jesus our Lord' (Rom. 8:38–9).

In this chapter we have considered three guidelines for coming to know Christ: firstly, that we should contemplate him in his humanity, because it is only through his humanity that we can glimpse his divinity; and secondly, that when we look at Christ of the Gospels, we should pray to recognize in him our own self-portrait, for we are called to become 'other

Christs'. Most of the chapter was given to the third guideline. We considered the key characteristic of Christ's personality, namely, his relationship to his Father, expressed in his human relationships in a life of sharing, a life for others. We are called to this same life-style both in our relationship to God and to other human beings. When we look at this truth we become more aware of the conflict within ourselves, between our relationship to God, expressed in a life of sharing and of compassion with other human beings, and our relationship with Mammon. We examined this conflict in the light of St Ignatius' Meditation on the Two Standards. This led us to the third guideline, namely, that whenever we pray to Christ, we should pray to share his spirit of poverty, for it is in so far as we share his spirit of poverty that we begin to discover the treasure within us, his presence.

In the next chapter we shall look at him present within us through his passion and resurrection.

Exercise

This is a small selection of Gospel texts suited to imaginative contemplation.

The infancy and hidden life
Luke 1:26–38   The message to Mary that she is to bear a
    child. Christ is still coming to birth in you and me.
Luke 1:46–55   Mary's delight in her poverty: 'My spirit
    delights in God my saviour.'
Luke 2:1–20   The birth of Christ.
Luke 2:22–35   Jesus is presented in the Temple, and Simeon
    takes the child in his arms and prophesies. The prophecy
    is still being fulfilled in us.
Luke 2:41–52   Jesus is found in the Temple. 'I must be about
    the affairs of my Father' – the theme of his life and of
    ours, which causes a row even in the most perfect of
    families!

The public life
Matthew 3:13–17   Jesus leaves home for the Jordan. Walk
    with him. Jesus is baptized. We are plunged into that
    same life. Hear the Father still saying to you, 'You are
    my beloved.'

Matthew 4:1–11 Jesus is tempted in the desert. His temptations are ours too.

John 2:1–12 The first miracle at Cana.

Luke 4:16–30 Jesus at first welcomed, then rejected at Nazareth.

John 1:35–51 The call of the first disciples.

Luke 5:1–11 The call of Peter.

Luke 11:1–13 Jesus at prayer.

Luke 6:17–49 Jesus preaching.

Luke 10:38–42 Jesus with friends – Martha and Mary.

John 4:1–42 Jesus and the outsider – with the woman at the well.

Matthew 14:13–21 Jesus feeds the five thousand.

Matthew 14:22–33 Jesus walks on the water. (The water symbolizes all the powers of chaos and destruction.) Jesus calls, 'Courage, it is I, don't be frightened.' He is still calling to us, 'Come'.

11

His Passion and Resurrection in Our Lives

Let him easter in us, be a dayspring to the dimness of us, be a crimson-cresseted east.

(G. M. Hopkins, 'The Wreck of the Deutschland')

Many, who can contemplate imaginatively on Christ's life, find it difficult to contemplate him in his passion. Their minds go blank, or they are overcome with guilt feelings, or afflicted with a sadness verging on despair. Their distress may arise from two very different reasons: false notions of the meaning of the passion, or it may be that they are sharing in Christ's passion at a deeper level than ever before.

In contemplating the passion, as in any other event of the Gospels, put yourself in the scene as though it were happening at this moment, yourself present in it. Be there as though you were seeing the scene for the first time, so that you see Christ the man, the carpenter's son from Nazareth.

Just as we can have false images of God, seeing him as monstrous Uncle George, so too we can approach the passion with similarly distorted ideas. In some preaching and teaching on the passion and death of Christ, a most hideous picture emerges of God, the Father, whose voracious appetite for vengeance – called retributive justice – can only be satisfied by the last drop of his Son's blood, drawn from him in the agony of crucifixion. Those on whom such teaching is inflicted then conclude that if they are to be accepted by the Father, they must also placate him with their suffering, and the more they suffer, the happier the Father will be. There was a type of hagiography which confirmed this depraved picture of God, depicting the saints as men and women, and the occasional child, dedicated to intense suffering and who, not satisfied with the sufferings which ordinary life imposed, added other torments of their own devising, flagellating themselves, rolling in nettles, standing reciting the psalms in ice-cold water, sleeping little and then only on the floor and living on a diet of bread and water. The false impression is then given that the more we suffer, the more we become like Christ and therefore the more pleasing to the Father. The directions for our journey through life can then be reduced to the simple prescription: 'Make life as difficult and painful for yourself as possible: the more you deny yourself in all things, the more you will find God.' It was this kind of picture of God and of Christ which revealed itself to Fred's imagination when he pictured Christ at Cana, seated on a high-backed chair, wearing a white robe, a crown of thorns, holding a staff and looking disapproving. Such a picture of God and Christ is not Good News, but a nightmare, does not strengthen and console, but weakens and terrifies, does not engender a love of God, but implants a religious schizophrenia in the psyche.

This deformed notion of the passion divinizes suffering which, in itself, is an evil and to be avoided. Suffering does not save: its effect is normally to destroy. Passively and indiscriminately to accept all suffering, as though in so doing we were imitating Christ, can be a denial of Christ. If we are victims of injustice and oppression and deceit, whether from secular or religious authorities, then to accept it passively and encourage others to do the same 'for the love of Christ' is to collude with evil, not to resist it. Christians must resist evil with all their power, but they must still try to love the evil-doers however difficult that may be, and, I believe, their resistance must never be violent.

In contemplating Christ, the man, in his passion, we must beg him to teach us, through his humanity and the pain of it, who God is. God, in Christ, is manifesting his nature in the sufferings of Christ. Therefore the God who holds me in being at this moment is a God who enters into my pain, and the pain of the world. He put aside his divinity and became a slave out of love for us (cf. Phil. 2:6–7).

In his life on earth, Jesus lived the love of his Father for all creation, manifested the Father's compassion and tenderness, the Father's love for the least of his creatures, his hatred and anger at every form of injustice and oppression. Image of the Father's goodness, Jesus antagonized and threatened those whose security consisted in the oppression and enslavement of others. Jesus saw the injustice and deceit being practised on the poor and helpless. He saw how the face of his Father was masked for the people by the multiplication of trivial rules and regulations imposed on them by religious rulers in God's name. Jesus did not choose to suffer this kind of abuse passively: he challenged the rulers and spoke out against them.

The opposition to him grew, the opposition of sin, of those who would not let God be God. God, in Christ, had the power to eliminate all opposition. 'Do you think that I cannot appeal to my Father who would promptly send more than twelve legions of angels to my defence?' (Matt. 26:53). God, in Christ, does not eliminate his enemies. He protests against their injustice and their hypocrisy, and uncovers their deceit, but he does not distance himself from them. God, in Christ, takes the pain of their sinfulness upon himself. It is as though all the accumulated power of evil, the hatred, greed and cruelty of humanity had joined forces and hurled itself at God, in Christ. 'He became sin for us,' Paul says.

In Christ, who is God, human sin and God's goodness meet in the same person. Christ absorbs the pain in himself and prays, 'Father forgive them'. When human sin had done its worst, God, in Christ, replies with the blood and water from his pierced side. God's love is greater than human hatred and has won a victory for ever. This is the triumph and the joy of the cross. Evil has been confronted, has been allowed to do its worst to God in the humanity of Christ, and God, in Christ, transforms this evil act into victory through love.

When we contemplate Christ in his passion, we do so not simply to recall a historical event now over and done with, but to encounter the living God, the God who enters our darkness, weakness and sinfulness, who enters our hatred and our despair, and can transform it. We contemplate the ravaged body of the dead Christ to understand the nature of God now holding me in being, a God who pursues us into our darkness and destructiveness, and entering and sharing it, brings life out of our death. Therefore we can take our own suffering, from whatever source it comes, whether physical illness, or bereavement, or the damage we have done to ourselves and the damage inflicted on us by others, or the pain we experience in letting God's pity, compassion and love act in us. In our pain we meet Christ in his passion, know his presence and healing power bringing hope out of our despair.

Contemplating Christ's suffering in his passion, the grandeur and the scale of it, our suffering can seem so mean in comparison that we feel we cannot possibly be sharing in his passion. We may see, with very painful clarity, that most of our suffering comes to us not because our lives are dedicated to promoting Christ's kingdom, but from frustration at our failure to build our own kingdom of wealth, honour and power, from knowledge of our own incompetence, feelings of inferiority, from physical weakness or mental slowness, from difficulties of temperament, loneliness, inability to love or be loved, in which there is no glory, no heroism, just a pathetic mediocrity. God, in Christ, meets us in all our pain and suffering, however mean and mediocre we may be. If we can have the humility to present this suffering to him in prayer, our weakness and mediocrity will be changed into the cause of our joy, for in our weakness we shall find his strength, 'For it is when I am weak that I am strong' (2 Cor. 12:10).

The love of God for us and for all creation is being revealed in the sufferings of Christ. We are called to answer this love, not by passive suffering, but by letting the love and compassion of God and his hunger for justice express itself in our own lives. If we enter into the passion of Christ, we begin to feel the pain of this world as Christ did, and his Spirit at work in us takes this pain, absorbs it, and answers it with forgiveness and love.

We would prefer a different kind of God, a God who would hurl back the pain onto those who inflicted it, adding a bit more to deter them from ever trying the same again, but 'God's foolishness is wiser than human wisdom, and God's weakness is stronger than human strength' (1 Cor 1:25).

It is not uncommon for people who contemplate the passion, and who do so without any preconceived or distorted notion of its meaning, to experience dryness, desolation and inner darkness, a sense of estrangement from God and disturbing temptations against faith, although they have prayed to be with Christ in his passion. In fact, they are with him, suffering his 'hour and the hour of darkness', sharing his sadness and his 'becoming sin for us', the experience which made him cry out, 'My God, my God, why have you forsaken me?' The pain they experience and the emptiness is the obverse side of their longing for God. If they were not so close to him, they would not feel so keenly the pain of his absence. They have no sensible awareness of his nearness, but the reality of his presence manifests itself in the changing quality of their lives, in a deepening and broadening love, joy, peace, patience, tolerance and goodness.

I hope I have not given the impression that unless we contemplate the passion, death and resurrection of Christ imaginatively, we cannot share in it. Every celebration of the Eucharist is a celebration of the life, passion, death and resurrection of Christ in which all creation is involved and taken up.

> As he [Christ] is the Beginning, he was first to be born from the dead, so that he should be first in every way; because God wanted all perfection to be found in him and all things to be reconciled through him and for him, everything in heaven and everything on earth, when he made peace by his death on the cross. (Col. 1:18–20)

The same God who manifested himself in the historical Jesus once-for-all is still giving himself to us in love through the signs and symbols of bread and wine. God is not time- and space-conditioned. The once-for-all action of God on Calvary is a continuous action throughout creation. In celebrating the Eucharist, we are celebrating our awareness of this tremendous truth.

As our sinfulness can infect and deform our image of God and our understanding of Christ's passion, death and resurrection, so too, it can distort our understanding of the Eucharist. Instead of a celebration which fills us with joy and wonder, broadening our vision and uniting us with ourselves and with all creation, the Eucharist can become a cold and formal ritual, performed mechanically with more attention to rubrics and money-raising than to God or to one another, and attended by many because they are afraid that their absence might cause their eternal damnation. Christian communities can be divided into hostile factions over the choice of hymns, the place of the tabernacle in the Church, the manner of distributing and receiving Holy Communion, who should and should not be allowed to receive it, or whether the Peace of Christ should be given to one another by the congregation! I am not saying that these questions do not have their importance, nor am I advocating abolition of all rubrics, rules and regulations, but I am saying that many of the questions which absorb our attention are very secondary. They preoccupy and divide us within the Catholic Church and between the Christian Churches, because our vision and understanding of the Eucharist is too limited; we turn this symbol of the reality of God's love for all his creation into a sacred object, a thing, and we do not allow God to be God to us even in this most simple and wonderful sign.

The Eucharist is given to us so that Christ's presence may be real in the lives of his people, a presence living in our attitudes and values, in our thinking, speaking and the style of life we choose to live. It is important that we should show great reverence to Christ in the sacrament of the Eucharist, but it is even more important that we should let his presence be real in our lives, for that is the reason he has given us the Eucharist, 'so that you may copy what I have done to you' (John 13:15).

We are all branches of the one vine, cells of the one body, which is Christ. The reality of his presence must be expressed in the way we communicate with one another, our mutual care and concern, whatever form it may take. Christ's presence is not real in a congregation, however religious they may be individually, whose members remain strangers or, still worse, enemies to one another. Nor can he really be present in a congregation whose energies and interests are focussed on themselves, and who do not show, as a body and as individuals, an interest and compassion for the needs of the immediate neighbourhood, and a consciousness that the congregation exists, as a Christian group, to serve the needs of others. As the presence of Christ becomes real in a congregation, it will show itself in the openness of that congregation to all people, of all religions and none, of all races, nationalities and classes in society, but it will have a special care for those whom the rest of society overlooks and despises. In this way, the congregation really is living in the presence of Christ, in the power of his passion, death and resurrection.

As with every other event of Christ's life, the resurrection is a mystery, and therefore we can never adequately understand it. Many Christians who say, 'I cannot believe in the resurrection any more,' are really saying, 'I can no longer accept the infantile notion of the resurrection, which once I could accept without difficulty,' and what they fear may be a loss of faith is very often an invitation to grow into a more adult faith. Because resurrection is a mystery, therefore God alone can teach us what it means and lead us into this truth in which we are living, moving and have our being.

As with the passion narrative, so too, we should approach the Gospels' resurrection accounts without, as far as possible, any preconceived ideas of its theological meaning, simply putting ourselves in the Gospel scenes and begging to know the joy of Christ's resurrection.

The content of our belief in the resurrection is not merely that Jesus of Nazareth, who was crucified, rose from the dead and appeared to some of his friends in bodily form, but that this Jesus is the Lord of all creation. This is a truth which cannot be obtained, or deduced, from any number of apparitions, however dramatic: it can only be known by faith. In St John's account, Peter and John are pictured running to the tomb on Easter Sunday morning. John arrives first, sees the empty tomb and the linen cloths lying there, but does not go in. Peter enters, John follows and 'he saw and he believed'. Before any appearance, John believed. Later in his Gospel John describes Thomas's doubts (John 20:28–9). Christ appears and says to Thomas: 'Put your finger here; look, here are my hands. Give me your hand, put it into my side. Doubt no longer, but believe'. Thomas replies, 'My Lord and my God,' a statement of faith, not a deduction from the evidence of his senses.

That Jesus Christ is Lord of all creation cannot be proved by reason: it can only be known by faith. The resurrection of Christ, Lord of all creation, is as new and as real today as it was two thousand years ago. Through the medium of the Gospel accounts and through the celebration of the Eucharist, we can be taken up in this mystery in which all creation lives.

The Gospel accounts of the resurrection do not together

give a coherent picture, and they contradict each other in parts. They are struggling to express in human language an event which transcends our categories of thought and imagination, of space and time. However, although there are inconsistencies in the details of the resurrection appearances, there are three common features and these are important for our understanding of how the resurrection is affecting our lives now.

The first common feature is that those to whom Christ appears are portrayed as being in a negative mood of some kind or other: the women in Mark's Gospel are terrified out of their wits; the disciples on the road to Emmaus are sad and disillusioned; Mary Magdalen is distraught; the disciples in the upper room are afraid and living behind closed doors; Thomas is in doubt. This suggests a truth which subsequent Christian experience confirms, that we can only come to know the risen Christ when we have experienced some kind of death, some disillusionment with ourselves and others, some loss, bereavement, sense of fear, hopelessness or meaninglessness and have not tried to anaesthetize ourselves against it. The answer is in the pain, which is revealing to us our poverty and our need of God. If we can acknowledge and be still in our poverty, Christ will show himself to us in his glory.

A second feature common to the Gospels' resurrection accounts is the slowness of those to whom Christ appears to recognize that it is the risen Christ. The disciples on the road to Emmaus have walked several miles with him before they recognize him, and Mary Magdalen mistakes the risen Christ for the gardener. This is also a feature common to our own faith in his resurrection, a slow dawning of the truth that he is a living presence in every detail of our lives. At first the resurrection is presented to us as an event outside of ourselves, something which happened two thousand years ago. Slowly, if our faith is developing, we come to know the resurrection as something which is happening to us now. The risen Christ is continuously coming through the closed doors of our minds and imagination as he came through the doors of the room where the disciples were gathered for fear of the Jews. He enters our consciousness, closed through fear of ourselves and our fear of other people, and says to us, 'Peace be to you'. The power of his resurrection gives us hope in a situation where before we felt it was hopeless, gives us courage to face a task when before we wanted to run away, gives us the ability and strength to be open and vulnerable when before we could think of nothing but our own protection and security.

A final feature common to the resurrection accounts is that those to whom Christ appears are commissioned to go and tell others. 'As the Father sent me, so am I sending you' (John 20:21). 'Go, therefore, make disciples of all nations' (Matt. 28:19). The Acts of the Apostles are an account of the resurrection, of the Spirit of the risen Christ at work in the early Christian communities, a Spirit of forgiveness and reconciliation, a Spirit of joy and peace even in the midst of conflict and persecution, a Spirit which breaks down the barriers between Jew and Gentile, slave and freeman, men and women, a Spirit summed up in this brief account of the early Church:

> The whole group of believers was united, heart and soul; no one claimed for his own use anything he had, as everything they owned was held in common. The apostles continued to testify to the resurrection of the Lord Jesus with great power, and they were all given great respect. None of their members was ever in want, as all those who owned land or houses would sell them, and bring the money from them to present it to the apostles; it was then distributed to any members who might be in need. (Acts 4:32–5)

Even if you cannot find the time, space or peace to contemplate the life of Christ imaginatively, never be disheartened. At the end of the day, as you recall the events of it, let Christ be in the room with you and hear him say, 'Peace be to you', showing his hands and feet, sign of his passion and death in which he has overcome all the powers of evil and destruction, so that there is no crisis you can experience, whether through your own or other peoples' fault, in which he is not with you, leading you to a deepening knowledge of the power and the glory of his resurrection.

When we hear Christ say, 'Peace be to you', how are we to know that we are not deceiving ourselves, conjuring up a Christ in our own image and likeness, who cries, ' "Peace, peace", when there is no peace', an imaginary Christ who confirms us in our prejudices and strengthens us in our obstinacy? The next chapter offers some guidelines in answer to this question and ends with a few brief comments on decision-making, based on the Spiritual Exercises of St Ignatius.

Here is some background reading, apart from the passion and resurrection accounts in the Gospels, which can be helpful in contemplating the passion, death and resurrection:

The last supper: Psalms 113–118 (which were recited at the Passover meal).

The agony in the garden: Hebrews 4:14—5:10.

Jesus' arrest and trial: Psalms 35, 38; 40, 55, 57, 64, 69, 70, 102, 142, 143; Isaiah 50:4–7, 52:13—53:12.

Way of the cross: Psalms 55, 72; Colossians 1:15–20.

Crucifixion: Psalms 22, 31, 88; Philippians 2:6–8; 2 Corinthians 5:7–18.

Taking down from the cross and burial: Psalms 42, 74, 130; Isaiah 42:1–9; 1 Corinthians 1:17–31; Hebrews 9:11–28; Wisdom 3:1–9, 4:7–15.

Resurrection: Psalms 2, 8, 19, 24, 62, 116, 118; Isaiah 30:18–26, 35:1–10, 43:8–13; Ephesians 1:15–23; 2 Corinthians 1:3–7.

12

The Decision in Every Decision – God or Mammon

God is at work in all things and therefore in every experience of our lives, in both joy and sadness, peace and agitation, pleasure and pain, but this statement, while it is true and can give us confidence in our dark moments, does not tell us how we are to react to these inner experiences. In wartime especially, but at other times too, we can do terrible things to ourselves and others. In doing so we may experience great inner revulsion, but either resist it, or anaesthetize ourselves against it because of an overriding categorical imperative which we call 'duty', or 'God's will'. How do we know it is God's will and not some destructive 'ought' operating within us? This brings us to a first guideline:

1. *It is characteristic of God to give true happiness and spiritual joy, banishing sadness and agitation.*
   It is characteristic of the destructive spirit to lead us to distrust this happiness and joy by false and subtle arguments.

This is an important general principle. The characteristic of God's action is happiness and spiritual joy, and therefore it should be the characteristic quality of the Christian whose life is directed to the praise, reverence and service of God. The destructive spirit brings sadness and disturbance and offers clever and subtle reasons for keeping us in this state.

True happiness and spiritual joy does not mean living on a perpetual 'high', but may be compared to the ballast in a ship. With ballast the ship will roll in a storm, just as a person capable of true happiness and joy will feel pain in a crisis, but the storm will not capsize the boat which will quickly right itself, even when struck by a wave. Similarly,

137

true happiness and spiritual joy does not mean living on a continuous high, unaffected by grief, sadness or loss, the pain of others, but it does mean that we shall not sink into despair under the blows, but will recover peace and tranquillity when the storm is over.

Therefore, if in a particular action or decision we feel great inner revulsion, destructive of inner peace and joy, then this cannot be from God and we need to look at and pray over the 'ought', or the notion of God's will which is operating within us. If our state in life, whether it be our health, married or Religious state, or our work leaves us in a constant state of sadness and anxiety, we must not divinize this state by calling it God's will and so accept it passively, but pray to know what it is in us that is blocking out the peace and joy which God wants to give us. He may be calling us to change our state of life, or to change the way in which we are living it.

What I have written may upset readers who do live more or less permanently in a state of sadness or depression. God is with you in your darkness and what I have written is to assure you that he is with you. I believe this, but it is not just a personal belief: it is the belief of the Church. But that he is with you does not therefore mean that you have to stay where you are. He is the God of true consolation, and therefore he is calling you out of your sadness and depression.

For those who are afflicted with gloom, it is good to pray and imaginatively contemplate the raising of Lazarus in John 11. Have a good look at Lazarus in his tomb. He is dead, corrupting, enclosed in darkness. Then hear the voice outside the tomb saying: 'I am the resurrection. If anyone believes in me, even though he dies he will live, and whoever lives and believes in me will never die.' Without forcing anything, let your own feelings of sadness and depression surface in your consciousness so that you see yourself locked within the tomb of your own sadness. Then hear the stone being removed and hear the voice of Jesus calling you by name, '. . . , arise, come forth'. Sometimes, people who pray in this way discover that they do not want to emerge from the tomb. This is not failure, but an important discovery, showing them that they are in the tomb of sadness not because God wills them to be there, but because they have chosen to be there for some reason. If this were to happen to you, do not be alarmed, but acknowledge your own attachment to the tomb and keep asking Christ to set you free.

Although the normal characteristic of the destructive spirit is to cause sadness and anxiety, it can sometimes attack more subtly by giving false consolation, peace, joy, enthusiasm; so this brings us to a second guideline:

2. *True consolation can be distinguished from false consolation by its results. If the consolation is false, the thoughts arising from it will tend towards something evil, or less good, and so lead eventually to disquiet, sadness, etc. In true consolation, the thoughts arising will tend to what is good.*

At the time, true consolation may be indistinguishable from false: the difference will only become apparent later. Two people may, for example, feel strongly moved by a sense of God's justice. Let us suppose that in one of them the consolation is from God, in the other from the destructive spirit. In their subjective feeling of being moved by a sense of God's justice there is no perceptible difference in the consolation they experience, and they are both right in accepting it, and trusting it is from God, but they should also notice the tendency of the thoughts which arise from it. The difference between true and false consolation will only become perceptible to them through the thoughts and actions which follow. If the destructive spirit was the cause of the consolation, then the thoughts and decisions which follow will gradually reveal themselves as destructive. The individual who is falsely inspired in this way may set to work with great enthusiasm but, in his or her zeal for a more just world, may begin to act contemptuously and destructively towards any unfortunates who do not share their world vision! There is a wealth of evidence in the history of the Church of the existence of false consolation and of the destructiveness that can follow if it is not spotted. Monsignor Ronald Knox's *Enthusiasm* is a detailed study of this point.

The daily examination of consciousness, already described on p. 77, is a good way of guarding against false consolation. In true consolation there will be a gradual increase of love, joy, peace, patience, kindness, goodness, trustfulness and self-control. There is also laughter, merriment and a lightness of touch when God is present. Solemnity, grimness, over-seriousness and frantic hurriedness do not bear the mark of God's action. Worrying and agonizing as to whether we are acting out of true, or of false, consolation is destructive, so we must relinquish the agonizing and trust in God's goodness. If we really are on a wrong course, he will make it clear to us in a way we can understand.

The rest of this chapter is an application of these guidelines, together with the guidelines given in chapter 8, to our decisions in life, because it is through our decisions that we determine the direction our lives shall take.

The decisions include major decisions of life, job, career, whether to marry and whom, or not marry, whether to enter Religious life, become a priest, but also include decisions within a way of life, how to live within this marriage, or Religious vocation, how to carry out this job or career, or, for many today, how to live in unemployment or in retirement, or alone.

If we want to make a decision according to God's will, which, as we have already seen, is to make the decision which our deepest self really wants, then the direction of our lives must be the praise, reverence and service of God, so that in the strength of that desire we can, if necessary, let go our attachment to any created thing. In other words, our decisions will be according to God's will only in so far as we are detached/indifferent to the alternatives before us. This detachment/indifference to the alternative choices before us is the heart of the matter in all Christian decision-making. Unless there is this indifference, the decision cannot be God's will and no number of techniques can make it so.

For example, you are offered a new job with increased salary. The world's answer is, 'Take it quick'. Faced with this choice, we feel the attachment to the extra money and we know this is influencing our choice. Then we must try to live and act as though we did not want the money, as though we were content with what we have, praying even not to have the extra money. This may sound very harsh. The object is not to predetermine the decision, but to ensure that the decision is made freely and for God, rather than solely for the increase in salary. The ultimate and right decision may be to accept the new job.

Sometimes we know, beyond any shadow of doubt, the decision we must take, whether in a major or a minor matter. It is as though the decision were already made in us. This is not an uncommon experience in people who experience a religious conversion or a call to priesthood or Religious life. However, once this decision has been taken and acted upon, they will have to make many other decisions, perhaps about matters which they had never even considered before, if they are to live true to their conversion or call experience.

More frequently, when faced with decisions, it is not immediately obvious what we should do. No amount of prayer can excuse us from doing our homework on the question but, assuming the homework has been done as efficiently as possible, we should then take the decision into prayer, asking God that whatever we choose it may be for his greater praise, reverence and service. We may be able to discover the choice we should make by noting over a period of time the effect a provisional decision has both on prayer and on our moods outside of prayer. If consistently in prayer and after it I experience desolation with this provisional decision, for example to accept a particular job, but find consolation in the alternative, then I should choose the alternative which brings the consolation.

If this method does not help because we feel at peace with whichever alternative we consider, then there is a further method, which may also be used to confirm a decision reached through the experience of consolation/desolation. Having prayed for a spirit of detachment so that my decision may not be made in the interests of my selfish-self and labelled 'God's will', I then draw up two columns on a sheet of paper. The first column is 'Acceptance of X', whatever X may stand for, and the second column is headed 'Non-acceptance of X'. I then subdivide each column into two divisions. Under 'Acceptance of X' I write in one column 'Advantages and Benefits', and in the other 'Disadvantages and Dangers' and I make the same division under the heading 'Non-acceptance of X', so that there are now four columns. Having filled in the columns, I consider which alternative seems the more reasonable and I decide accordingly, offering the decision in prayer and asking God to confirm it, if it is for his greater glory and praise. An alternative, or additional method is to

141

imagine what advice I would give to a friend who might come to consult me with an identical problem or, imagining myself to be at the moment of death, I then ask which decision I would then want to have taken.

People are often deterred from even attempting these methods because they feel sure they can never have the detachment necessary to make such a decision. What is important is not that we should have reached a state of complete detachment, but that we desire to have this state and struggle towards it. Others, having tried these methods and reached what they consider afterwards to have been a 'wrong' decision, give up trying. To act in this way is to have misunderstood the purpose of these methods. They are not presented as fool-proof ways of reaching 'correct' decisions, but as methods of growing more perceptive and responsive to the action of God in our lives.

We shall now apply what has been said about individual decision-making to decisions made by a group of people.

Why is it that so many movements and organisations spring up within the Church and within society from a noble and generous purpose, attract intelligent and conscientious people, flourish briefly, then become so preoccupied with questions of internal organization that their original purpose is forgotten, and they die? The same question could be asked of the Church itself. Starting with a small group of frightened men in a closed room, the movement exploded into the Roman world until it became the official religion of the Empire. It has been beset ever since with questions of internal administration, organization, levels of authority, a problem summed up in the twentieth century by one of the bishops at the Second Vatican Council who declared the Church to be crippled with its own 'triumphalism, clericalism and legalism'.

The Church must have organization, structures, a teaching authority, laws, but (as we saw in chapter 2) undue emphasis on the institutional element of the Church, to the detriment of the critical and mystical, cripples, leaving her so preoccupied with the problem of her own maintenance that her mission to the world is neglected and the inner life of her members, where the true wealth of the Church lies, is stifled.

The crises which afflict the Church today – dwindling

numbers, disaffection and division among its members – are a blessing if we can react to the problems in faith. The Church is being called to purify herself of all her disordered and subtle attachments to false securities, to wealth, honour, pomp, power and prestige, in order to rediscover her true meaning as a sign, and an effective sign, of the power of the risen Christ, a Christ whose power was shown in powerlessness, a Christ with a special love for the poor and the oppressed, a Christ who was vulnerable to the pain of this world, absorbed it in himself, and who replied to it with forgiveness. There are many signs that the Church, in its members in many different parts of the world, is responding to God's call.

Our own subtle attachments to idols are at their most effective in our individual and group decision-making, and they can be so subtle that we are not even aware of them. To illustrate this point I shall give a caricature, deliberately exaggerated to illustrate how secretly and effectively our idols affect our decisions, whether they are made on our own behalf, or on behalf of others. The example is a parish council meeting, but the hidden forces operating beneath the spoken words are the same forces which operate in every group decision, whether it be a Vatican council, a State cabinet meeting or a tenants' association gathering. I shall give the minutes of the meeting summarizing the comments of each member, then in brackets I shall give the truth behind the spoken words. If the bracketed comments seem cynical, it is to make the point that hidden agenda can operate in every group. In this particular group there is perhaps more destructive hidden agenda than usual.

Minutes of the St Jude's Parish Council
6.00 p.m., 10 November 1985

Present: Rev. P. Simon (parish priest)
Mr W. Oxbridge (headmaster of St Jude's Comprehensive School)
Miss G. Grey (retired headmistress of St Jude's Primary School)
Miss MacPhail (senior mistress, St Jude's Primary School)
Mr S. Springer (youth officer)

Mr A. Fisher (local councillor, publicity convenor)
Mr McCollum (bank manager)

The minutes of the October 10th meeting were read and approved. The council then discussed the first point on the agenda: 'Now that planning permission has been granted, a site chosen and bank loan assured, are we to go ahead with the building of a parish youth club?'

Rev. P. Simon: Welcomed the suggestion, but advised postponement of any decision because afraid the enterprise might overtax both the finances and energies of the parish. Also questioned whether a youth club was the best service the parish could give to its youth and to the cause of ecumenism, which should be a priority in all our Church ministry.

(Rev. P. Simon is feeling his advanced middle age, is still hoping for a bishopric and is afraid of any move which may involve him in financial risk or more work. He can no longer communicate with modern youth.)

Miss Grey: Agreed with Father. Finds modern youth too pampered. Thinks organized voluntary work in the town would do them more good and save money for worthier causes.

(Miss Grey's new bungalow and extensive garden, which needs clearing and digging, adjoins the site of the proposed club. Her peace is threatened.)

Mr Oxbridge: Agreed with previous speakers, considers the town already adequately provided with youth clubs, besides the excellent facilities which the school provides. Clear religious instruction for youth a greater need than billiard and pool tables.

(Mr Oxbridge is an ambitious man whose life revolves around O- and A-level successes. He will oppose anything which could distract his pupils from their studies.)

Miss MacPhail: Thinks that a youth club is badly needed, illustrating her point with many examples. Suggested the youths themselves should be taught how to build it and that the club should be open to all religions. Building the club would bring unity among the youth, would give them a sense of pride, appreciation of the value of work and practice in ecumenism.

(Miss MacPhail's life has been blighted for the last twenty years with a consuming hatred for Miss Grey, who was appointed headmistress instead of herself. What Miss Grey proposes, Miss MacPhail must oppose.)

Mr Springer: Agreed with Miss MacPhail on the need for a youth club, a need confirmed in his own experience as a professional youth worker. Advised strongly the appointment of a professionally qualified and adequately salaried youth worker for the club. In making this suggestion, he also stated that he had no personal interest in such a post.

(Mr Springer, just engaged, is afraid that he would be expected to run the youth club unsalaried in his spare time.)

Mr Fisher: Enthusiastic about the project and assured the meeting that a Catholic club would be welcomed by the town councillors and that it would not be an unecumenical gesture. Optimistic that the club could be built through Manpower Services, which could cut costs and provide a work force.

(Mr Fisher is ambitious for higher things and hopes to enter national politics. He approves anything which can bring him publicity.)

Mr McCollum: Voted in favour of the club.

(Mr McCollum looks after the parish accounts voluntarily. He dreads the extra work which would be involved, but reckons the youth club would serve a need and therefore does not allow his reluctance to face extra work to influence his vote.)

The arguments given by the members of the parish council for and against the proposal are not in themselves bad but, under the appearance of good and sound proposals, all the members, except for Mr McCollum, are intent on furthering their own personal kingdom. Fr Simon's predominant interest, to which everything else is subordinate, is his own comfort and chances of promotion, Miss Grey has dedicated her life to peaceful retirement, Mr Oxbridge to examination successes, Miss MacPhail to revenge, Mr Springer is afraid of being imposed upon and Mr Fisher's idol is favourable publicity for himself. Whether they decide on a youth club or not is relatively unimportant, because their attitude, if it continues unchanged, will ensure that the youth of the parish, and any other groups they may consider, will be neglected, the good of others being subordinated to their own private interests. In their outward behaviour and with their lips they have the interest of the community at heart; in reality, they are using the community for their own praise, reverence and service. In words they serve: in practice they exploit. They are worshipping Mammon.

We all share the defects of the members of this parish council. In what follows I shall suggest some ways of detecting and countering our subtle hidden agendas when we are making group or community decisions. The method proposed is more suitable for serious policy decisions of a group or organization rather than for details of administration. No amount of prayer, goodwill, faithful adherence to the method proposed, can excuse the decision-makers from having to work out a clear formulation of the proposal and from doing careful homework before they reach the decision stage.

After his conversion, Inigo of Loyola went to Paris University to study and there he collected a group of friends who shared his ideals. The whole group decided they would go together on pilgrimage to the Holy Land. In Paris, only one of the group, Pierre Favre, was a priest. While waiting to go to Jerusalem the rest of them were ordained priests. Because of war with the Turks they could not make their pilgrimage, and so they went to Rome and offered their services to the Pope, because they wanted to serve in the Church wherever the need was greatest and they thought the Pope to be the most likely person to know those needs. As they were a very talented group, their services were in great demand and they were invited to work in different parts of Italy and beyond. The group was likely to disintegrate and so they had to reach a decision. They broke down the decision initially into two questions, 'Are we to remain united as a group?' and 'Are we to take a vow of obedience to one of our number?', which was another way of asking, 'Are we to become a religious order within the Church?' At the end of a day's work they met regularly to consider these questions. On the first question, 'Are we to remain united as a group?' they had no difficulty in reaching a unanimous decision, but when they began to consider the second question, they could not reach agreement even after three days, so they broke off for a few days to pray and fast before meeting again, but this time they devised a new method. Each in turn was asked to give his reasons against taking a vow of obedience. The rest listened in silence and there was no argument. When everyone had given their reasons against the proposal, they all went off to pray. They then considered the reasons for the proposal in the same manner and prayed over these. Finally, they met to give their decision. They were unanimous in their agreement to take a vow of obedience to one of their number.

To sum up this method briefly: The fundamental disposition of all who take part in the decision-making must be the desire to praise, reverence and serve God, as explained in chapter 5. It is that fundamental disposition which says, 'Thy Kingdom come, not mine: Thy Will be done, not mine,' so that we are prepared to let go any attachment which, in this particular decision, may be in opposition to God's kingdom. Without this fundamental disposition, there can be no true discernment of God's will.

What if I think that neither I, nor the rest of the group, possess this fundamental disposition? The temptation is then to abandon all effort to discern God's will. No individual, still less any group, is likely to have attained complete detachment. What is important is that we desire and pray for that spirit in reaching this particular decision. Growth in detachment, like growth in anything else, is slow. On the analogy of a journey on foot, particular decisions made in a spirit of detachment are steps along the road to God. The whole journey consists of separate steps. There is an annual hopping procession in Luxemburg with two backward hops for every three hops forward, a good image of our progress towards God.

Once the proposal has been formulated, then let each speak against it while the others listen, and there is no discussion on the points raised except, perhaps, to ask for clarification.

After each has spoken it is good to have a few moments of silence to reflect on what has been said.

The reasons against the proposal are then taken into the prayer of each one and after the prayer, they should note their inner feelings of consolation or desolation. The reason is that if rejection of the proposal is according to God's will, then the reasons against it, being pondered, are likely to resonate in the feelings, bringing a sense of peace and tranquillity. If the reasons against the decision are contrary to God's will, then they are likely to register in the feelings with a sense of unease, agitation or anxiety.

Then the reasons in favour of the proposal are given in similar fashion and prayed over. Finally, members are asked to give their decision.

Although this method may seem very simple, it is, in fact, more complicated and difficult in practice, but this should not deter us from trying it.

The method is difficult and complicated because we are difficult and complicated creatures with layers upon layers of consciousness. As the prophet Jeremiah wrote, 'The heart is more devious than any other thing, perverse, too. Who can pierce its secrets?' Our real agenda in a meeting may be hidden not only from others, but also from ourselves. The struggle for indifference and detachment is a lifelong struggle for all of us. The temptation is to give up any attempt to practise group discernment, because the group is most unlikely to reach that state of detachment which true discernment demands. There are two important points to be remembered in answer to this temptation. The first is that although we may not have reached a state of detachment over against all created things, we may reach a state of detachment over a particular thing in a particular decision. Mr McCollum, for example, may not have been totally detached, but on the question of the youth club he was able to recognize and overcome his own reluctance to take on extra work. The second point is that the practice of discernment is not primarily to enable us to reach 'the right decision' – that is, one which we never need to revoke – but to increase our sensitivity and responsiveness to God at work in every detail of our lives. We are more likely to choose according to God's will if we attempt this method than if we ignore it.

In the next and final chapter I shall apply some of the ideas we have been considering to the danger which threatens every human being today, the extinction of human life on earth by nuclear war.

13

The Valley Speaks – God and the Nuclear Threat

> You and I are one undivided Person.
> (from an ancient homily for Holy Saturday)

God is not only at work in every particle of his creation and in all our human experience, but he makes his home in us. He is our treasure, hidden within our own experience. There is no fear, no darkness, no despair, no pain of ours which he does not share. He is constantly reaching out to us, not because we have been good, virtuous, respectable or hard-working, but because he loves all that he has created and his living Spirit is in all. We meet him in our fear of nuclear war. If we can face the fear, we shall find him closer to us than we are to ourselves. If we refuse to consider the problem, we ignore the voice of God speaking to us through the facts of his creation. A spirituality which insulates and anaesthetizes us against the pain and terror of this world is an idolatrous spirituality, because the God whom we worship is the God of compassion who took our griefs upon himself in Christ.

I shall look at the nuclear problem through an imaginary conversation from a tower-room window, where I lived for eight years in St Beuno's, a Jesuit Centre of Spirituality in North Wales, the house in which the poet Gerard Manley Hopkins lived and wrote 'The Wreck of the Deutschland':

> Away in the loveable west,
> On a pastoral forehead of Wales,
> I was under a roof here, I was at rest,
> And they the prey of the gales . . .

My window faced west across the beautiful Vale of Clwyd,

'Woods, waters, meadows, combes, vales . . .' and, in the distance, lay the mountains of Snowdonia, their outline like a giant warrior at rest.

The conversation is imaginary, but it expresses truths which have slowly broken through some of the layers of my cocooned mind in the course of the last forty years. The conversation leads me to reflect and then to reach conclusions which are not the conclusions of the majority of Christians, nor of the majority of Roman Catholics, nor of all my fellow Jesuits. None of us has a monopoly of truth: each sees from an individual point of view, our vision affected by every incident of our unique past. That is why we have such a need of each other. I do not expect readers to agree with my conclusions, but simply present my own conviction. I realize that subtle forms of self-deceit, self-glorification, or hidden aggressivity may influence my conclusions, but I also know that this fear must not deter me, or anyone else, from bearing witness within the Church to what I think and feel. I do so, trusting that, if I am wrong, God will eventually show me my deceits.

In spare moments at St Beuno's I loved to stand at the window of my tower room and look out over the Clwyd valley. One day I found myself talking to it! When I was in a bad mood over something, angry or irritated, fearful or worried, I used to say to the valley, 'Take it,' and I would hurl the lot out of the window. The valley did not explode, but smiled as serenely as ever. It was as though the valley could share my pain and even absorb it, forging a link between us, restoring a measure of peace, until I could smile back and begin to see the pettiness of my inner tantrums. When in a good mood, glad and grateful for someone or something, the valley could re-echo my joy. It became for me a symbol of God, his sacrament, sign and effective sign of his presence and of his ways with us, for he shares our pain, absorbs it, and offers his peace in return, and he is the joy of our desiring. The valley also became a symbol of his immensity, his beauty, his creative power and a manifestation of his glory, which is his hidden presence breaking through in his creation.

But I could also look at the valley in a very different way, seeing it as a scorched wasteland, a bleak desert, lifeless, motionless save for the white ash falling gently on its charred remains, and see this happening not only in the Clwyd valley, but in every valley and hill, every town and city of our world, a nightmare vision which could become reality at any moment. This is not alarmist exaggeration: it is the truth. Although we cannot afford food or water for many millions of people of the Third World, we have enough explosives to ensure the equivalent of two tons of TNT for each living person.

After gazing on the valley in this way, prayers uttered in calm, well modulated tones in a comfortable church, 'Dear Lord, grant us peace,' sounded hollow and useless. Such prayers should be screamed, but at what kind of God, who can allow such a horrendous possibility? How real is our talk of God's goodness if he can allow all human life, our struggles, hopes and dreams, all the beauty, delicacy and intricacy of his creation to end so hideously? Is all our prayer and spirituality a desperate attempt at make-believe because the reality is too horrible to contemplate? Is all our talk about a loving God false, and are our own protestations of love for him and for others really only a muffled scream, a desperate attempt to save our skin?

The last paragraph summarizes years of doubt and darkness lurking deep in my consciousness, usually well repressed, but breaking through every now and again in black moods, in anger and disillusion at the impregnable complacency of the Church in some of its official pronouncements, at the unreality of so much preaching and teaching, which seems content to ignore, or even to justify and support the demonic activities of the powers and dominions of this world, giving the Church's blessing, for example, to nuclear submarines while condemning those who practise contraception, accusing those priests and Religious who try to come to grips with the evils of our time of betraying the true spirituality of the Gospel and labelling those who question the economic and social structures of Western democracy of being Marxist. There were times when I looked out of the window and cried in my heart, 'Christ, where are you?'

At such times the valley, like God, was silent. 'You and I are one undivided Person.' The voice came from within. I knew its literary source, an anonymous Christian writer who imagined Christ, after his death, going to the gates of hell

and saying these words to Adam. I would look at the valley
and hear variations on these words: 'You and I are one
undivided Person'; 'You and I'; 'You are in me and I am in
you'; 'Be at home in me as I am at home in you'. A momen-
tary flood of delight would sweep away my unbelief until I
steadied myself, ignored the valley and addressed myself. 'Be
sensible. You are allowing yourself to be carried away by a
woolly nature mysticism, probably caused by overtiredness.'
The solemn voice of moral conscience would then confirm the
judgement of common sense, 'You know you are fickle, vain,
stupid, a hopeless mixture of belief and unbelief, as resolute
and stable as those autumn leaves swirling in the wind. Ignore
the vapourings of a tired imagination, stop wasting time
dreaming and get down to some solid work.' Fortunately, I
often dithered, and then I heard, 'Who is the greater, you or
I, your sinfulness or my goodness, your fickleness or my
faithfulness, your stupidity or my wisdom?'

As these words sank into me, I began to glimpse something
of my own deviousness and of the falsity of my common sense
and moral conscience, which forced my attention away from
the valley to attend to me, seeking security within the prison
walls of reason and rectitude apart from God. I would see,
momentarily, that the God who calls me through the valley
is the God of all creation, the God who dwells in all that
exists, the God who put aside his divinity and became a slave
for me and for all creation, God who takes upon himself the
pain of the world. The truth is not that I want to behave
sensibly and with moral probity: the real truth is that I cannot
face the God of compassion who shares the world's pain,
and so I scuttle away from him. Had my circumstances of
upbringing been different, I might have tried to escape in
other ways, through drink or drugs, or by finding security in
wealth or status, but I have chosen the escape route of
religious respectability. 'The heart is more devious than any
other thing, perverse, too. Who can pierce its secrets?' Idolatry is still the basic sin. I catch a glimpse of my own idolatry,
my dedication to self-preservation apart from God. Although
I call upon his name, I am using his name to protect me from
his presence. 'Nothing so masks the face of God as religion.'

I begin to understand better something of my black moods,
of my anger and frustration at certain kinds of ecclesiastical

preaching and teaching, at the closed complacency of some in the Church, at cosy liturgies in which we pray for solutions to the world's problems without any acknowledgement that we may be contributing to them. I begin to see that I am raging against myself, for a part of me hungers for God, yet another part frustrates this hunger by searching for its own self-made security to which it gives the name of God. God is still speaking to us as he spoke to Israel through his prophet Isaiah, 'When you stretch out your hands, I turn my eyes away. You may multiply your prayers, I will not listen. . . . Search for justice, help the oppressed' (Isaiah 1).

I begin to see that the real battle is not in working to change the structure of the Church and of society, but in struggling to change the structure of my own psyche. This may sound very individualistic and selfish, but the only thing we can change is ourselves, for the only power that can bring creative change is God. I cannot domesticate God, I cannot tell him what to do, no matter how noble the cause: all I can do is let his glory through in me, let God be God in my own life.

I look again at the scorched, lifeless valley, and now I see it as a symbol of myself and of every other human being apart from God. The fear of meaninglessness, of nothingness, haunts us all. With all the strength that is in us we fight this fear, try to hide it from ourselves, build up a security to protect ourselves from it. When our security is threatened, we defend it with every means in our power. Fear makes us do terrible things to one another. Rats in panic are more considerate of each other than human beings. Yet this very fear, if we can face it, can become our salvation.

Apart from God, we are the scorched valley. My self-made security, which keeps out the God of compassion, becomes the means of my destruction. 'Unless you lose your life, you cannot find it.' There is no security except in God, who is love, and who loves all that he has made. Our salvation is in loving and cherishing his creation, in so living that others may have life. There is no other salvation: only the scorched valley. Ignatius, as we have seen, expressed this truth in the phrase, 'Man is created to praise, reverence and serve God and by this means to save his soul'. The majority of mankind may not know or acknowledge the Christian God by name, but they meet him in their own hearts when they feed the hungry, give drink to the thirsty, shelter the homeless, relieve the suffering, show understanding, act justly and live with integrity. God weeps and loves in them. They go out to God when they show compassion, they reject him when they grow callous to human suffering by so concentrating on their own security and well-being that they are willing to risk millions of lives and hold millions in subjection in order to obtain it.

Our Western defence policy is a terrifying illustration of the truth that our self-made security is the means of our destruction. We project our corporate fears of annihilation onto an enemy, currently the Soviet Union, our glorious allies of forty years ago. We pile up our nuclear arms, point them towards the Soviet Union and believe, in our blindness, that we are defending ourselves, not realizing that the real enemy is within us, successfully destroying us by the very means we use for our defence. Supposing, and it is a very unlikely supposition, that our nuclear arms were to succeed in ridding us of the Soviet threat, how long would it take before we found another enemy? We would then start on another cold war, build up our arsenals again and use the same lying propaganda to justify our actions. Until we face the real enemy, the holocaust is bound to come sooner or later.

But surely, we must defend our lives and the life of our nation against tyranny? Certainly we must, but we must first ensure that we have identified the real tyrant, and we must never defend ourselves with nuclear arms, which can destroy our world forever. 'But before you make statements like that', says the Christian philosopher, 'you must first prove that nuclear arms are wrong in themselves.' I took this argument, as I have taken all the other arguments justifying possession of the nuclear deterrent, to the valley. As the white ash falls, the philosopher's arguments do not sound convincing, but the devastated valley raises a question for the philosopher. 'What is the value of the criterion you propose, and what are its limits?'

Then I ask the valley about the other arguments for the deterrent proposed by its Christian supporters. 'We must face the fact', they argue, 'that we are living in a sinful world, that there are evil men and evil governments who hold human life cheap and are quite prepared to destroy any who will not accept their ideology.' The valley remains non-committal: it has seen all the generations of men come and go and knows only too well the truth of the argument so far. 'Today', the argument continues, 'we are faced in the West with an enemy pledged to world domination. Our Christian heritage, our democratic way of life, our freedom of speech and of religious worship are all being threatened. Are we quietly to succumb, ourselves and future generations, to atheistic Communism? We abhor the deterrent; we would much rather not have it, but we are created to be free and we must, as our forefathers did before us, be ready to risk our lives for the sake of freedom. Because we live in a sinful world, we are forced to choose between two evils, the evil of Soviet domination on the one hand, and the evil of possessing the nuclear deterrent on the other, which, we hope, we shall never have to use and which has, thank God, preserved us for the last forty years. Those Christians who favour nuclear disarmament and who join CND – the majority of whose membership, be it noted, are non-believers – are spineless Christians who have lost touch with their Christian heritage and have adopted a vague humanism in its place. Because they do not appreciate their faith and its tradition, they are not prepared to fight for it. They are blinkered idiots, liable to upset the balance of power and so make nuclear war the more likely.'

The valley remains silent: it can no longer answer, but contemplating the horror of it, I hear other voices:

> Yes, you love all that exists, you hold nothing of what you have made in abhorrence, for had you hated anything, you would not have formed it. And how, had you not willed it, could a thing persist, how be conserved if not called forth by you? You spare all things because all things are yours, Lord, lover of life, you whose imperishable spirit is in all. (Wisdom 11:24–7)

Then another voice, 'In my name you have exterminated millions who are precious in my eyes, whom I honour, for whom I died. You fled from me in life because you could not tolerate my love for all creation. Depart from me: I do not know you, for you have preferred your security to my glory'.

Where is the real enemy? The real enemy is within each of us. It is our fear of God, the God of all creation, the God of compassion, who shares the pain of this world. As a nation we reject this God, preferring the God of our own security. We elect the government most likely to ensure our continued security in affluence. Politicians know this, and so the economy becomes the central issue in our democratic elections. We do not question the sources of our wealth, nor bother to inquire whether our affluence is won at the cost of other peoples' oppression and misery. Part of our wealth comes from our export of arms to the rulers of Third World countries, arms of reliable quality and destructive power which can effectively silence the cries of the poor and oppressed. Within our own country the economy rules and we consider this O.K.

Deeper and more pernicious than our greed is our false sense of self-importance as a nation. Unable to afford money for the sick and ageing and homeless in Britain, or for the starving abroad, we can quickly muster large sums of money and pay a vast cost in human life to uphold what we call 'our sovereignty'. We allow a nation which oppresses the poor of Central America to place its death-dealing weapons in our land, which they may shoot off without our permission, while we threaten to shoot any who dare to approach this new 'Holy of Holies'. This policy of greed and pride we wrap up in a package called 'The Defence of Freedom', defend it with weapons which can destroy the earth, and pray God's blessing on our endeavours.

As I gazed upon the valley, I knew that our policy of nuclear deterrence is a blasphemy, an expression of our atheism. The enemy is not Russia, but our own greed and self-importance. As Christians we must not say, 'I believe in God,' unless we can also say,' and I renounce every form of self-defence which threatens the lives of our generation and of all future generations'. God is the God of life who loves all that he has created, not the savage destroyer and exterminator.

As I write, I am conscious of many friends and acquaintances whom I respect and whom I consider better Christians than I, but who still believe in the value of the nuclear deterrent. In asserting that they are mistaken and that their views on the nuclear deterrent arise out of the atheist part of themselves, I acknowledge the mystery of God's workings and that they can be much nearer to God than I. God can speak through the jawbone of an ass, but it does not follow that the ass ceases to be an ass or is in any way superior to those to whom the words are addressed!

If you are a believer in the value of the nuclear deterrent, then give time to gazing at the beauty and delicacy of God's creation. Look at its valleys and hills, its towns and cities, into the eyes of the world's children, then speak to Christ hanging on the cross and tell him that in his name and for his greater glory you feel compelled to risk destroying everyone and everything you see and hope to see, in defence of our Western values. Do this daily and hear what Christ your teacher says in reply through the feelings and emotions which arise in you through this exercise.

The nuclear menace is a fact. The facts are kind: God is in the facts. That is why we must give attention to them, contemplate them and beg God to teach us what this horrific threat of nuclear destruction is saying to us. Nuclear weapons are the expression of attitudes of mind and heart, of fear, greed, callousness. We are called not only to rid ourselves of nuclear arms, but of the attitudes which produce them. We are being called to a radical revolution of mind and heart, so that we begin to see our national security is in sharing, not in hoarding, our welfare is in a spirit of co-operation, not of ruthless competition, is in cherishing nature, not in exploiting it, in trying to understand rather than in condemning, in recognizing the dignity of each human being rather than in rating their value by their earning power or their rank in society.

When we face the question of nuclear arms and of violence, of which nuclear war is the ultimate expression, the vastness, complexity and apparent insolubility of the problem can overwhelm us, as though we are trying to stop with our bare hands a vast destructive juggernaut moving inexorably towards us. The temptation is either to join the majority, jump on the juggernaut, and proceed along the road of our own and other peoples' destruction, or to bury our heads in the sand either by ignoring the problem, or by concocting a spirituality which will assure us that we, along with evangelical fundamentalists in the United States who are such strong supporters of nuclear arms, will be safely and cosily 'enraptured' by Christ when the Armaggeddon, for which we have worked so faithfully, consumes and obliterates the rest of mankind.

God is calling us to a radical conversion and to a depth of trust in him which will allow his power to be released in our weakness, his wisdom to be revealed in our bewilderment, his truth to break through our disillusion. As the atomic nucleus has to split before the nuclear power can be released, so our cocooned ways of thinking and acting in society and in the Church have to break down before the energy and creative power of God can be released. Then we shall be able to say with St Paul:

I shall be very happy to make my weaknesses my special boast so that the power of Christ may stay over me, and that is why I am quite content with my weaknesses, and with insults, hardships, persecutions, and the agonies I go through for Christ's sake. For it is when I am weak that I am strong. (2 Cor. 12:9–10)

Epilogue

Most of this book was written on the Isle of Skye, where I lived from March until July 1984 in a room behind the Catholic Church in Portree. Writing is often a painful occupation, especially when a day's work produces pages of scored-out scribble and the mind feels like an emptied tube of toothpaste. I was greatly helped in these periods by remembering Angus, aged four years, who often came to Mass with his mother. Mass would hardly have begun before Angus was snoring quietly in his mother's arms, waking at the end to help clear the altar and bring the water and wine cruets to the sacristy where liquorice-allsorts were also stored. His heart had no lofty ambitions and his eyes did not look too high. He was not concerned with great affairs or marvels beyond his scope. It was enough for him to keep his soul tranquil and quiet as he slept in his mother's arms, content in the knowledge that there would be something to eat when he woke up!

As I remembered Angus, I would recall Psalm 131 and this would bring me back to the heart of the matter, the truth of things, that we live, and move, and have our being enveloped within the goodness of God and that our treasure is in the living awareness of this truth.

In reading this book you may have felt sometimes, 'How complicated he makes it; can't he keep it simple?' The answer, briefly, is that we are complicated creatures, but to find a pathway through the tangled labyrinthine ways of our conscious and unconscious selves, our attitude of heart must be simple. Whenever you feel confused, bewildered, disillusioned, frightened, be childlike in your trust in God, present and beckoning you in the chaos. In trusting with your heart, it is as though you put your hand in his and let him lead you.

When the Lord has given you the bread of suffering and the water of distress, he who is your teacher will hide no longer, and you will see your teacher with your own eyes. Whether you turn to right or left, your ears will hear these words behind you, 'This is the way, follow it'. (Isaiah 30:20–1)

God is in all things, so that there is no particle in creation and no experience of yours in which he is not with you. That is why any spirituality which cocoons us from the pain of this world, or which declares that the Church should keep out of politics and social justice questions, is a false spirituality and an idolatry. Certainly, the Church must never identify itself with any particular political party, but to say that the Church must keep out of politics is to assert that the ways in which we relate as human beings is outside the scope of religion. Politics is concerned with some of the structural ways in which we relate to other human beings. Religion is concerned with all the ways in which we relate to others, because it is in those relationships that we relate to God. In his description of the Final Judgement, which is happening in the here and now, Christ says to those who ignored the hungry, thirsty, naked and imprisoned, 'I tell you solemnly, in so far as you neglected to do this to one of the least of these, you neglected to do it to me' (Matt. 25:45).

In speaking of our relationship to God and to Christ we have to make use of analogies, but no analogy is ever adequate. We speak of 'Christ living in our hearts' and 'making his home in us', and such analogies are useful, but it is more true to say, 'We must live in the heart of God, we must make our home in Christ,' a heart which is always greater than anything we can think or imagine, a home that embraces the whole Universe. That is why St Catherine of Genoa once made this extraordinary statement, 'My God is me, nor do I recognize any other me except my God himself.'

This final prayer can help us to make our home in Christ rather than restrict him to our own narrow quarters. Whenever I say it, I shall remember those who read this book and ask you to remember me. The prayer comes at the end of St Ignatius' Spiritual Exercises:

Take Lord and receive all my liberty, my memory, my

understanding and my will, all that I have and possess. Everything I have is yours, for you have given it all to me; to you I return it. Take me, Lord, and do what you like with me, only give me your grace and your love, for that is enough for me. Amen.